God's Word is ministe... ...
It is perfect
true & right

MW00414549

MELISSA DEMING

SWEETER
THAN
HONEY

CULTIVATING AN APPETITE
FOR THE WORD OF GOD

A Discipleship Series

Sweeter than Honey: Cultivating an Appetite for the Word of God

© 2016 by Melissa Deming

Editing by Amanda Williams and Diane King.

To our sweet Savior who sets the divine table

before us and invites us to feast

BOOKS IN THIS SERIES

Crowned: Created for Glory, Called by His Name
(2015)

Sweeter than Honey: Cultivating an Appetite
for the Word of God
(2016)

Kingdom Hearts: Becoming a Servant Who
Looks and Lives like the King
(2017)

TABLE OF CONTENTS

INTRODUCTION

This is the book I needed in high school and college – not simply a book explaining *how* to read and apply God's Word to my life, but a book on *how* and *why* only the Word of God can satisfy the deepest hunger pangs of the heart of a young woman.

While in seminary in Wake Forest, N.C., I discovered Howard Hendricks' much-loved classic, *Living by the Book*, and it changed how I approached God's Word. (In fact, his system forms the basis of this book.) Having grown up in a Southern Baptist church and a home steeped in the language of faith, Hendricks' Bible study methods were easily digestible to me. But as our culture rapidly transitions away from its Judeo-Christian roots toward a secular society with the Bible belt having all but vanished, the stories of many of the women in our church pews are often quite different from mine. More and more, women are entering the doors of our churches or attending our women's ministry events lacking both a biblical worldview and a biblical background (often through no fault of their own). Many are starving for the meat of the gospel, yet know not how to prepare a meal for themselves –

1

much less for others. And instead of giving them hands-on cooking lessons that start with the basics, we've become accustomed to handing out ready-to-eat dinners in prepackaged containers (think video-driven Bible studies). Ask any busy woman, microwavable meals on takeout trays pale in comparison to hot, home-cooked meals enjoyed around a table bursting with friends and family.

This material started out as one such hands-on "cooking" lesson for the women of Living Faith Community Church, a Southern Baptist church plant in Pittsburgh – a congregation full of bright women hungry for God's Word. *Sweeter than Honey* is the second of three discipleship classes specifically written for unchurched women – women who claim no church home. I published the first book in the series, *Crowned: Created for Glory, Called by His Name*, last year. The third book on missional living, *Kingdom Hearts: Becoming a Servant Who Looks and Lives Like the King*, is forthcoming. I cannot say thank you enough to the women of Living Faith for giving me the indescribable gift of providing me a front row seat to watch their transformation and growth as disciples of Christ unfold.

Sweeter than Honey is a five-week discipleship book on how to study God's Word, but most importantly, it is meant to be used as a guide to help women teach other women how to feast on the Scriptures, as well. This book is both for the woman who can't boil water, per se, and the woman responsible for all those Pinterest-level culinary masterpieces! (We see you journaling and lettering in your Bible!) But no matter our "cooking" level, we all benefit from a refresher course on mastering the basics of Bible study. For that reason, this book can be read individually but works best in a small group context.

For the Student

You do not need a seminary degree to sit at the Master's table. When Jesus called his first followers, he picked men who were sitting in fishing boats and tax offices, not classrooms. Acts 4:13 tells us, *"Now when they saw the boldness of Peter and John, and perceived that they were <u>uneducated</u>, <u>common men</u>, they were astonished. And they recognized that they had been with Jesus"* (emphasis mine).

The people marveled at how much Peter and John knew of the Scriptures because they were considered to be "uneducated" according to the proper religious traditions. Yet, Peter later became the disciple Christ chose to build his church (Matt. 16:18). John became one of the most prolific writers of the New Testament! (He wrote one Gospel, the letters 1, 2, and 3 John, and the book of Revelation). Despite their upbringing and past experiences, these men grew to be spiritual heavyweights. How can that be? These men were qualified to speak about spiritual things not because of any special giftings, but because they "had been with Jesus," who is the Living Word of God. The Word of God shaped them into his very image, and that is his heart for you, too. Jesus invites us to feast with him as we are, knowing that the more we enjoy his table the more we will grow in wisdom and understanding.[1] So, please don't delay in digging into God's Word because you feel ill-equipped or unskilled. As Peter and John demonstrate to us, every disciple starts from the beginning; it is Christ who transforms them by his Spirit and through his Word.

Dear new student of the Bible, you are capable of reading God's Word and, with his Spirit's help, understanding and responding to its timeless truths. You simply need the commitment to sit down with Christ at his table each day and an open heart and mind to try some of the new dishes he has provided. If you find that breaking out of your daily routines and pushing past your comfort zone is your biggest hindrance to growing in Christ, you are not alone! Find a friend to bring with you to the feast and you can hold each other accountable as you dig into God's Word together. I encourage you to open his Book without fear, but rather, with a spirit of excitement to see what he reveals to you about himself. I promise that once you've tasted of our Savior's sweetness, you will be forever changed!

If you aren't sure if you've ever tasted of the Savior's sweetness, then please turn to the very back of the book before you get started. I'd very much like to introduce you to my Savior. He's got a seat of honor reserved just for you.

For the Teacher

This book was written for you, too – for the mature believer who has opportunities to disciple the women around her but doesn't know where to begin. Inside you won't find a guide on parsing Greek verbs or step-by-step instructions on in-depth word studies. Important as those things are, your disciple likely cannot digest those foods, yet. (Maybe we'll save those steak dinners for a follow-up book?) Your first challenge in teaching women to grow their appetite for God's Word will be to instill in them their need for its daily nourishment despite busy schedules and comprehension level. As their appetite grows, you can add in additional layers you believe to be beneficial.

Ideally, a more experienced "chef" or mature believer would walk a disciple through the basics of Bible study I've outlined in this book, helping her put her new study techniques into practice and culminating your time together with a 31-day Bible reading challenge. Additionally, each chapter contains a "Feast with Me" section written specifically for leaders and teachers offering simple ideas for helping your disciples learn how to view and handle God's Word.

On my site, I offer several free downloads for small groups. The free PDF leader's guide contains answers and aids for many of the discussion questions at the end of each chapter. The "Bee Truthful" questionnaire is also available for download to better gauge how well and often the women in your group study God's Word. Print and distribute these cards on the first day of your study and ask them to fill them out anonymously. Never assume your ladies are reading and understanding the Scriptures or that you know the reasons they are or are not.

Also on my site, I've provided ideas for hosting this material as part of your next women's event. Both the brevity of the book and the hands-on learning opportunities are easily tailored to use for a women's weekend retreat or training event.

All that is needed is a woman of the Word willing to teach other women how to study God's Word. Above all, I hope this book helps you encourage and equip the women around you to feast on God's Word each day and invite others to his lavish table.

Melissa Deming
2016

7 *The law of the Lord is perfect,*
reviving the soul;
the testimony of the Lord is sure,
making wise the simple;

8 *the precepts of the Lord are right,*
rejoicing the heart;
the commandment of the Lord is pure,
enlightening the eyes;

9 *the fear of the Lord is clean,*
enduring forever;
the rules of the Lord are true,
and righteous altogether.

10 *More to be desired are they than gold,*
even much fine gold;
sweeter also than honey
and drippings of the honeycomb.

11 *Moreover, by them is your servant warned;*
in keeping them there is great reward.

12 *Who can discern his errors?*
Declare me innocent from hidden faults.

13 *Keep back your servant also from presumptuous sins;*
let them not have dominion over me!
Then I shall be blameless,
and innocent of great transgression.

14 *Let the words of my mouth and the meditation of my heart*
be acceptable in your sight,
O Lord, my rock and my redeemer.

Ps. 19:7-14

PART I:

Cultivating an Appetite
for the Word of God

BEE TRUTHFUL

1. **On the scale below, rate how well you feel you know and understand the Bible.**

    1 (novice) ------------------------- 4 ----------- 5 (pro)

2. **Circle one: how often do you read the Bible?**

    Rarely

    On special occasions

    Monthly

    Weekly

    (Daily)

3. **When you read the Bible, how long do spend reading at each sitting?**

5 minutes or less

15 minutes

30 minutes

1 hour+

4. **What is the biggest obstacle you experience in reading the Bible consistently?**

    I find it confusing

    I find it boring

    I find I'm too busy

    I don't know where to begin and get overwhelmed

    I have doubts about the Bible's accuracy

    I don't think it's relevant to my life

    I don't enjoy reading in general

    I read other biblical material
    devotional books - H in AiM
    teaching books
    nite devotional

5. **If you consistently read the Bible each day, what motivates you to do so?**

    Love the LORD
    Love reading it
    Growth   12
    HeLP others

Bee Truthful

1. On the scale below, rate how well you feel you know and understand the Bible.

(I'm a novice) 1 ● ● 5 (I'm a pro)

2. How often do you read the Bible? Circle one.

Almost never	Only in emergencies	Once a month
On Sundays	Every day	We're joined at the hip

3. When you read the Bible, how long do you spend reading at each sitting?

Less than 5 min ● ● 1 hour +
30 min

4. What is the biggest obstacle you experience in reading the Bible consistently each day?

☐ I find it confusing
☐ I don't know where to begin & get overwhelmed
☐ I have doubts about the Bible's accuracy
☐ I don't enjoy reading in general

☐ I find it boring
☐ I find I'm too busy
☐ I don't think it's relevant to my life
☐ I _____

5. If you consistently read the Bible each day, what motivates you to do so?

Download and print this survey at:
www.hiveresources.com/books/sweeterthanhoney

CHAPTER 1

GOD'S WORD IS SWEETER THAN HONEY

In the pages of this book, you will discover the secret ingredient for a happy, healthy life. It's not the type of secret ingredient that only works in the expert hands of the world's Martha Stewarts, who seemingly produce culinary masterpieces out of one-pot dishes. Nor is it the type of secret ingredient that you might have stumbled upon quite by accident while surfing for a substitution for cream of tartar. This is a secret that is available to all, yet known by few, and used rightly and consistently by even less.

Yet, it is a secret that promises to transform even the direst of baking catastrophes into a satisfying feast. This recipe for a happy, healthy life is meant to be consumed not only at our own table but presented on our finest platters to friends and family around us. This life-changing ingredient is God's Word, and it is truly "sweeter than honey."

Psalm 19 tells us that God's Word is more precious

and more meaningful than anything else we pursue in this life. As women, we tend to pursue a lot of things in this life - a lot of worthy things and a lot of unworthy things. Yet, God's Word stands above them all because it is, as the Psalmist declares, sweeter than honey.

In Scripture, honey takes on great significance. In the Old Testament, when God revealed himself personally to his people, Israel, he promised to give them a land flowing with "milk and honey" (Ex. 33:3). In both ancient Egypt and Israel, honey was prized both for its sweet taste and healing properties. Honey was a luxury, reserved for the social elite – pharaohs and the royal court.

In the twenty-first century, we don't have the same appreciation for honey as the ancient Egyptians or Israelites had. We ingest so many different kinds of sugary treats that our western palates have become oversaturated with sweetness. If you look on the baking aisle at your grocery store, you'll find all manner or means to sweeten your food – organic, artificial, chemical – most of which I can't pronounce much less spell. In our culture, we are crazy about our sugar.

When my boys were 3-years-old, I attempted a sugar-free diet for the family. I threw out all the cookies and candies. We cut out all processed foods. I even made my own peanut butter and (attempted) to bake my own bread. Shortly after our sugar-free experiment began, the world seemed to conspire against us. A well-meaning neighbor brought over homemade, organic chocolate nut clusters. Now, I wasn't about to tell someone who had slaved over organic chocolate for my minions, "Oh, sorry, we're cutting back."

Nope. Despite our new diet, I immediately handed that chocolate over to my kids so she could see the joy that came from the fruits of her labor. I thanked her profusely in the hope that one day she would taste the sweetness of our Savior. Needless to say, our diet was short-lived, but our friendship with our neighbors bloomed.

But if it's not sweet neighbors, it's birthday parties or class parties, it's Halloween or the sugar-coated checkout lane carefully constructed to give mothers everywhere panic attacks and larger receipts – you can't get away from sugar if you tried. Entire businesses and brands are geared around this one truth: our palates crave sweetness. But, here's the deal. With all the choices before us, we have lost sight of true sweetness. Even more importantly, our palates greatly influence our cravings and our appetites. Spiritually speaking, the same is true. Spiritually, we do not always crave what we should. The more junk food my kids eat, the more they crave it.

The Israelites knew that God's promise of a land flowing with milk and honey wasn't entirely about the milk or the honey. When God promised his people this lush land, he wasn't promising them simply prime real estate with a beehive out back so they could make a little money on the side or sweeten their tables. When God promised his people "a land," he was promising them a special and separate place where they might enjoy his presence and all the sweet benefits and blessings that come with knowing their Lord God in a personal way. Psalm 19 says God's Word is *"sweeter also than honey and the drippings of the honeycomb."*

Ladies, if you are going to take away one truth from

this book, I hope it's this: God's Word is capable of capturing our hearts and satisfying every desire we long for - pleasure, wisdom, well-being, beauty, comfort, wealth, security, position, prestige. God's Word is better than gobs of gold and sweeter than the best honey for a reason – *because it gives us a taste of God himself.*

I hope by this time you've had a chance to "bee truthful" and take the Bible reading questionnaire located at the beginning of this chapter. This is a time for you to evaluate your attitude toward God's Word. Do you crave God's Word, or do you crave other things more?

In this short study, we will discover exactly how sweet God's Word truly is and how we can cultivate an appetite to know God through his Word. We will also discover that our appetites determine everything. Psalm 19 tells us that our attitude and appetite for the Scriptures will determine the degree to which we love Christ and look like him.

WHAT IS GOD'S WORD?

So, let's turn in the Word to Psalm 19 and find out what God's Word is. In his powerful little book, *Reflections on the Psalms,* C.S. Lewis said that Psalm 19 is "the greatest poem in the Psalter."[2] There are 150 songs to choose from in the book of Psalms, so that's saying something!

Overall, Psalm 19 is a song about a God who wants to be known by his people and who makes himself known in several ways. The first part of this song says

God reveals himself to us through nature (vs. 1-6). When we look around the natural world, we see proof of God's existence and his involvement in his creation.

But there is a more specific way that God reveals himself. We don't just know about God through the skies, but also through the Scriptures. It is through his Word that God – the Creator of the Universe – speaks personally and clearly to you and me. In it, he tells us things we must know in order to live fully, eternally, peacefully, confidently, radiantly, and joyfully. He tells us who he is, he tells us who we are, and he tells us how we can become like him. God's Word is not just a dusty old book. God's Word is not just an important book. God's Word is God's Word about himself *to us*. Through the Scriptures, God speaks to each of us reading this book, even now.[3]

Since the Bible is God's personal Word to us about himself, let's take a look at what God is saying about himself. Now I'm going to put you to work. Read Psalm 19 and make some notes in the chart at the end of the chapter about the way God's Word is described beginning in vs. 7. Below are the descriptions I wrote down.

1. The <u>Law</u> of the Lord is <u>perfect</u>.

In verse 7a, the Psalmist says God's Law is perfect. Whose Law is perfect? God's Law. What is in these pages originated with God. The word Law is a "comprehensive term for God's revealed will."[4] Everything we read in the Bible is there because God revealed it to us. The word "perfect" literally means that it is complete, whole, and sound. It tells us everything we need to know in order to have a meaningful relationship with God. And because God is perfect, his revelation about himself is perfect, too. It contains no errors.

2. The testimony of the Lord is sure.

What the Bible says about God (its testimony about itself) is sure. In the original language, the word "sure" is very interesting. It means carries or supports, painting the picture of a Father or parent carrying a child. We can be sure of God's Word because it remains steady and constant even as the world around us shifts. Even as we encounter raging waves that threaten to wreck us, God's Word carries us through the storm.

Additionally, sure "...can mean not only what is firm" as in fixed, but also "what is confirmed or verified."[5] God's Word is sure in that it is faithful to the truth — truth that has been verified throughout history and confirmed by first-hand eyewitnesses. We can trust God's Word because it is sure.

3. The precepts of the Lord are right.

Verse 8 says the precepts of the Lord, his authoritative principles, are right. They are "morally right or straight."[6] God's Word won't lead us down a wrong or crooked path. So, God's Word is not just right (says right things, righteous things), but says right things *for us*. They offer us the right way to live. We'll talk more about that in the next chapter.

4. The commandment of the Lord is pure.

20

Verse 8 also says the commandment of the Lord, or God's general commands, is pure. It is not defiled by error or confusion. More specifically, it is clear about what and whom it testifies. We see this echoed in Prov. 30:5, which says, *"Every word of God is pure; He is a shield to those who put their trust in Him"* (NKJV).

5. The rules of the Lord are <u>true</u>, and <u>righteous</u> altogether.

Next, the Psalmist describes God's Word as true and righteous altogether. The rules or ordinances of the Lord refer to his social and civil judgments. In our society, we have a rules and statutes. Some are put into effect merely to serve political agendas, like executive orders and tax codes, but God's rules are not so. They are altogether true and righteous.

Because they are "truth," they carry his authority with them. This is important because our world says truth can neither be known nor judged. Our culture tells us that each person has the right to define truth on his or her own terms. The measure of this type of worldly truth becomes whether or not it brings offense to another group or individual. Essentially, when our version of truth bumps up against another person in an offensive way, it suddenly ceases to be truth. Per the world, truth is believed to originate from inside man; it is considered a subjective expression of something true, not an objective fact based on reality. Psalm 19, however, tells us the opposite. The Psalmist is emphatic that there is such a thing as objective, real truth. It exists in God's Word (his rules and ways), not in man, and most importantly, this truth can be known.

"Altogether" God's Word is righteous and true, meaning the entire contents of God's revelation forms a whole – and each part is true. So, we can't take bits we like from here or there while rejecting the parts of God's Word that seem offensive or outdated to modern sensibilities. Objective truth never expires. God's Word is true and righteous in its entirety and without exception.

So, what is God's Word? The 66 books of the Bible – all of it – is God's revelation of himself. And God's Word claims to be perfect, sure, right, pure, true, and righteous.

IS GOD'S WORD TRUSTWORTHY? (WHAT THE WORD SAYS)

Psalm 19 makes some very bold claims about God's Word. But can we believe those claims? Is God's Word really perfect, sure, right, pure, true, and righteous? Is it really that sweet? If we were to turn it over, what would we find on its nutritional label? Man-made stuff? Are Christians delusional when we claim we can know God objectively? *opinions based on facts and not feelings*

At the heart of each of these doubts is this central question: is the Word of God trustworthy? Let's start by letting the Bible answer that question for itself, because the Bible offers proof to bolster its claims that it is the real deal, that what's inside is authentic, and not manufactured.

Scholars use several terms to describe how Scripture testifies to its own trustworthiness. I like how author and pastor Kevin DeYoung categorizes these terms. In his helpful little book, *Taking God At His Word*, he uses the acronym S.C.A.N. The Bible is trustworthy because it is sufficient, clear, authoritative, and necessary.[7] That is an easy way to remember the answer to the question: "Is the Bible truly trustworthy?" Interestingly, we see each of these claims in Psalm 19.

1. The Bible is trustworthy because it is sufficient.

The Bible is trustworthy because it is sufficient. The sufficiency of Scripture is just a technical way of saying that the Word of God is enough. This is important because our culture says one of the reasons the Bible is untrustworthy is because it is insufficient for our time. According to the media and pop culture, the Bible is in need of an update on its views on everything from abortion and sexuality to personal autonomy. *how behave, being emotional & govern myself*

> **S – SUFFICIENT:** God's Word is enough. It doesn't need an update. It offers us everything we need in order to know God and his salvation.

But Psalm 19:8 says, *"The precepts of the Lord are right."* They won't let us down. They won't lead us astray from what is both right and what is right *for us*, and this is the important implication - it always stands as relevant. *relates to the times or situation*

2. The Bible is trustworthy because it is clear.

Second, God's Word is trustworthy not only because it is sufficient, but also because it is clear. Psalm 19:8 continues by saying, *"The commandment of the Lord is pure."* It is clear, or sincere.

> **C – CLEAR:** God's Word is clear. It doesn't need a translator. It offers clear and understandable teachings on God and his salvation.

Now, this doesn't mean there aren't difficult terms or passages in the Bible. Nor does it mean we will be able to understand everything the Bible says perfectly. The clarity of Scripture means each believer, due to the Spirit's work of illuminating the Scriptures in our hearts and minds, is capable of understanding what the Scriptures say without a human mediator or interpreter (John 14:24-26). (If you're interested in learning more about the Holy Spirit's role in illuminating the Scriptures, turn to the end of chapter 4).

Each believer, every woman reading this book, can understand enough of what is written in the Bible to grow and nourish herself on God's truth. Her ability to understand God's Word will grow over time, but overall, the Bible is not a mystery revealed to a select, privileged few.

3. The Bible is trustworthy because it is authoritative.

Scripture is trustworthy because it is sufficient, clear, and, third, because it is authoritative. God's Word is trustworthy because it comes from a trustwor-

24

thy source. God is the source of all truth (John 1:1, 14; 14:6; Ps. 25:5; 119:89). If we do not believe the Bible came from God, but rather is a collection of writings by men with no divine element, then it holds no authority over our lives.

> **A – AUTHORITATIVE:** God's Word comes from God. It has the final word over our lives.

Tragically, an increasing percentage of Americans do not believe the Bible is authoritative. A 2014 study called "The State of the Bible" conducted by the Barna Research Group found that an increasing percentage of Americans believe the Bible is just another book of good teachings (11 percent in 2007 to 18 percent in 2014).[8] I don't know about you, but I am not content to order my whole life around a book filled with good ideas or simply good teachings. I am only willing to order my life around a book that makes the audacious claim of Psalm 19:9: *"The rules of the Lord are true and righteous altogether"* (emphasis mine).

Because God is the source of truth, his Word is truth. When scholars speak of the authoritative nature of God's Word, they often say it is *inspired* by the Holy Spirit, or literally "God-breathed." This simply means the Holy Spirit, working in connection with specific men of his choosing throughout history, inspired them as to what and how they should write. Second Peter 1:21 says, *"For no prophecy was ever produced by the will of man, but men spoke from God as they were carried along by the Holy Spirit."* For those of you who are new to studying the Scriptures, this process may sound a bit squirrely. So, let's outline what inspiration isn't.

Inspiration isn't a light bulb. Inspiration cannot be reduced to an inspirational idea. The Holy Spirit actively breathed out God's Word into the hearts of the biblical writers. The active nature of his involvement demonstrates he was more committed to the process of divine inspiration than simply sending a virtual idea someone's way and then letting humans take his idea and run with it.

Inspiration isn't a voice recorder. The Holy Spirit did not dictate each and every word the writers were to use without taking into consideration their writing style, ability, and unique set of ministry perspectives. If the process of inspiration worked through dictation, then all 66 books of the Bible would sound the same. We know this isn't the case because Paul's letters to the early church don't sound like the poetic language used by the Psalmists. And the stories of the Old Testament patriarchs don't look or sound like the visions of the apostle John in the book of Revelation. The Holy Spirit did not offer us a recorded message, and the biblical authors weren't court room scribes or robots. The biblical process of inspiration was a dynamic, collaborative effort.

In 2 Peter 1:21, Peter says the biblical writers were "carried along by the Holy Spirit," suggesting an "assured outcome, one that is carried out and guaranteed by another."[9] The Bible originated in heaven. As a divine book, it is an authoritative book. But the Bible is also a human book, written by men of God who were guided in their message by the Spirit of God.

4. The Bible is trustworthy because it is necessary.

26

That thought brings us to our last point regarding the trustworthiness of Scripture. Not only is the Bible trustworthy because it sufficient, clear, and authoritative, but also because it is necessary. We can sit here all day and dream up what God must be like or act like, but no matter how hard we try or how imaginative we get, we cannot hope to know God with any sort of accuracy or objectiveness unless God first reveals himself to us. We need God's Word. We need it in order to know about God and know about our Savior. And the knowledge it gives us about God is perfect. That's the exact claim of Psalm 19:7: *"The Law of the Lord is perfect."*

N – NECESSARY: God's Word is necessary to know God. It offers what general revelation cannot – salvation in Christ Jesus.

The Bible claims it is *inerrant,* or without error. To say the Bible is inerrant is to affirm that the Bible in its original form is perfect; it contains no errors or mistakes. God's Word is fixed, steady, confirmed, sure (Ps. 19:7). Sometimes you will hear it as described as *infallible* (incapable of error).

We need the Bible to know who God is (perfect) and who we are (imperfect). And we need his perfect Word to us so that we can follow its ways, listen to its warnings, and order our entire lives around it. We will find out why in the next chapter, but above all, we must remember that the Bible is trustworthy because it is sufficient, clear, authoritative, and necessary.

IS THE BIBLE TRUSTWORTHY?

S – SUFFICIENT: God's Word is enough. It doesn't need an update. It offers us everything we need in order to know God and his salvation.

C – CLEAR: God's Word is clear. It doesn't need a translator. It offers clear and understandable teachings on God and his salvation.

A – AUTHORITATIVE: God's Word is from God. It gets the final word over our lives.

N – NECESSARY: God's Word is necessary to know God. It offers what general revelation cannot – his salvation.

IS GOD'S WORD TRUSTWORTHY? (WHAT THE WORLD SAYS)

The Word of God claims to be trustworthy, but our culture tells us something totally different. Our world tells us God's Word is foolish, contradictory, old-fashioned, and, therefore, untrustworthy. We are faced with those views every day. We hear it from our college professors, our kid's textbooks, our Washington representatives, and our friends' Facebook rants. Everyone is suddenly a Bible critic and a scholar.[10]

So, let's answer two of the most common objections to the trustworthiness of God's Word that we encounter in our world today. This is important stuff because if we buy into these cultural stingers, then we will never cultivate an appetite for God's Word.

Cultural Stinger #1: The Bible Isn't Accurate

Cultural Stinger #1 says since we don't have the original copies of the Bible (called the autographs) and the copies we do have are full of errors, we can't know if the Bible we have today is accurate. The world says we have no way of knowing if what we have *now* is truly an authentic and accurate account of what God said *then*.

This argument is really about the authenticity and accuracy of the transmission process – how accurately the Bible was copied over the years. Critics often use the example of the telephone game. They claim that as a message travels from person to person, it becomes garbled and tainted in the transmission process. The message one ends up with is drastically different from the original because the final message depends on the trustworthiness of the people passing the message along.

So, is what we have *now* what the biblical authors wrote *then*? Is the Bible accurate? Any answer to this question must take into account our basis for truth – it is God and his Spirit. If we trust that the Spirit of God inspired God's Word, then we must also trust that the same Spirit can adequately supervise it and safeguard its transmission through the centuries.

It is true that we don't have the original copies or autographs of the Bible. We don't know what happened to them. Perhaps in the Spirit's wisdom, he allowed them to slip from human hands knowing that man has a tendency to worship created things rather than his Creator. However, you can know and trust that the Bible you have in your hands today is an accurate translation of the holy Scriptures. But if you want some specific responses to this cultural stinger, I'll give you two.

Let's talk manuscripts

Can you guess how many manuscripts or fragments of the Bible we have? Today, we have over 5,700 manuscripts of the New Testament – and that's only counting Greek manuscripts! We have 10,000 more in Latin and about 1 million quotations of the Bible used by the church fathers in their letters to one another during the early church period. The manuscripts we have date as early as 100-150 A.D.!

This is why the number of manuscripts is important. We can take all those manuscripts, study them, see where they diverge from one another, and then come to an accurate translation of the Bible. But in case you still feel that we can't know what the original copies of the Bible said, consider by comparison the number of some other important historical documents that often go undisputed.

Roman historian Livy (Titus Livius) wrote 142 books on Roman history. Yet, only 35 manuscripts of his writings survived. Of his seminal piece, *History of Rome*, we only have a quarter. Imagine if we only had a quarter of the Bible! Yet we have copies of virtually every book in the Bible.

Tacitus is considered one of antiquity's greatest historians. He wrote 14 books, one of them being his

Annals, which refers to Christ and the persecution of Christians under the Emperor Nero. The survival rate of his works fared worse than Livy, with only 4-and-a-half manuscripts accounted for today.

Suetonius was the state librarian for the Emperor Trajan (98-117 A.D). It is from his works that we learn Nero supposedly fiddled while Rome burned. Two more accident historians Thucydides (an Athenian) and Herodotus (Greek) were both important figures predating Christ. Thucydides' 20 surviving manuscripts, which speak of the wars between Sparta and Athens and human nature in war, continue to be studied in universities around the world. Herodotus' systematic style of investigation earned him the title the Father of History of Western culture. Of his famous work, *The Histories,* only 75 manuscripts remain.

Compare those paltry figures to the number of manuscripts of the Bible. Not only do we have substantively more manuscripts of the Bible than any other ancient text, but our earliest manuscripts of the New Testament date to the second century. That means that the testimony of eyewitnesses to Jesus' life and ministry could be immediately recorded without too great a length of time passing.[11]

AN EMBARRASSMENT OF RICHES

HISTORIAN	OLDEST MANUSCRIPT	NUMBER OF MANUSCRIPTS
Livy (59 B.C. – 17 A.D.)	4th Century A.D.	35
Tacitus (56 – 120 A.D.)	9th Century A.D.	4 ½
Suetonius (69 – 140 A.D.)	9th Century A.D.	200+
Thucydides (460 – 400 B.C.)	1st Century A.D.	20
Herodotus (484 – 425 B.C.)	1st Century A.D.	75
NEW TESTAMENT	100-150 A.D.	5,700 Greek 10,000 Latin +1 million quotations
OLD TESTAMENT	3rd Century B.C.	Tens of thousands

The dating of our manuscripts shouldn't go without noting. I like to take pictures of notes the boys write me or post funny things they say to Facebook to ensure I won't forget. Even by the time my husband gets home from dinner, I've often already forgotten things I would have loved to share with him. Some things I want to forget, but can't. Overall, the more time that passes, the easier it is to forget what you heard - the exact words, the tone, or even the context surrounding a conversation. But because our copies begin during the time of Jesus and his disciples, we can be confident that we have an accurate and authentic rendering of Jesus' words and actions, context and tone.

As the chart indicates, New Testament writings are

more plentiful than any other copies of other ancient literature. We have a true "embarrassment of riches."[12]

Let's talk archaeology

If the number of manuscripts we currently have weren't enough, we keep discovering more and older manuscripts and fragments of Scripture!

In 1946, a Bedouin was looking for a lost sheep among the crumbling limestone cliffs east of Jerusalem. He threw a rock into a cave to determine if his sheep was inside, when he heard something crash. In the cave, he discovered several large clay jars, inside one was a piece of leather wrapped in linen. The man took the scroll and fragments to an antiquities dealer to see what he had uncovered in that cave. Do you know what it was? A scroll of the book of Isaiah – all 66 chapters – dating from 125 B.C. This discovery made it about 1,000 years older than the oldest manuscripts of the Hebrew Bible known at the time!

In 1952, they began excavation on this area and they uncovered a network of caves producing over 900 different texts in Hebrew, Aramaic, and Greek, of which 230 were biblical scrolls. They date from the 3rd century B.C. (200 B.C.) to 1 A.D and include partial and complete copies of every book in the Hebrew Bible (39), except the book of Esther. You might have heard of them as the Dead Sea Scrolls.[13] It has been deemed the greatest archaeological event of the twentieth century.

There are two things we should note about this discovery. First, the Dead Sea Scrolls confirmed the Hebrew text we had been using was a faithful representation of the original.[14] Scholars estimate about 95 percent of the text was identical to the Dead Sea Scrolls, and the 5 percent of variance consisted mostly of "slips of pen and variations in spelling."[15] So, let's give it up for the scribes, y'all, because sometimes Hebrew names are hard to spell and say. Let's be honest, in Sunday School we duck our heads so we don't have to read those long genealogical lists in the Old Testament. So, the scribes did a "supernatural" job in copying and transmitting the Bible's message. We can trust that the Bible we have now truly *is* what they wrote then.

Second, the Dead Sea Scrolls confirmed that as time progresses, we don't get farther away from the original message of the Bible, but the opposite! As time goes on, our translations get increasingly better due to advancements in textual criticism and the continued discovery of new fragments and copies of Scripture.

So, don't get stung by this cultural stinger that says the Bible is not accurate. Although we don't have the original copies of the Bible, we can trust that our present translation is an accurate account of what God said. The Word of God is indeed trustworthy.

Cultural Stinger #2: The Bible is irrelevant

Cultural Stinger #2 says the Bible was written by men with political agendas, so even if we do have an accurate and authentic copy of the original versions, the ideas it contains are old-fashioned, oppressive, and irrelevant for life today. At its heart, this stinger is an assault on the canonization of Scripture.

When we refer to the canon of Scripture, we mean the process by which each of the 66 books of the Bible were canonized, or confirmed to be authoritative. [16]

The word canon is taken from the Greek word *kanon,* meaning "rule" or "standard." Our culture says the Bible is untrustworthy because it is not from God, it was canonized, or made to be authoritative, by a group of men in Syria during the 6th century. So, our culture says the Bible isn't a really old ancient piece of history; rather, it is fairly new.[17]

But here's the problem with that view: the Scriptures were always considered holy and sacred even during the time of Jesus. In Luke 24:27, Jesus is walking and talking with some men. He walks the men through the Bible, and listen to what he says about it: *"And beginning at Moses and all the Prophets, He expounded to them in all the Scriptures the things concerning Himself."* Jesus believed the Bible was a book about him. Jesus believed since it was all about him, then all of it was accurate.[18]

Throughout history, the church was united in its belief that the Bible is a trustworthy source for knowing God. It wasn't until the 19th century that scholars, and society in general, began to doubt its trustworthiness. Their doubt originated not in any new discoveries that disproved the Bible, but in a seismic shift in thinking that denied the existence of miracles.[19] The Bible couldn't be true, they said, because miracles (the virgin birth, the resurrection, and more) weren't possible. As a result of this naturalistic worldview, the Bible was no longer seen as a historical record, but as a fabrication of men.

I don't know about you, but I'm not ready to throw out thousands of years of church history. I think I'll stick to the source. I'll stick to Jesus' view. So, don't get stung by the world! The Word of God, as we have it, is trustworthy. We have thousands of years of written history on our side, and we have the testimony of the Living Word Jesus Christ, himself.

CONCLUSION

We started this chapter by asking: what is God's Word? We discovered that God's Word is God's personal Word to us about himself. And it is perfect, sure, right, pure, true, and righteous altogether. In short, God's Word is a trustworthy source for knowing him.

HOW WAS THE CANON CONFIRMED?

In order to be considered Scripture, the book or letter in question had to pass several tests by providing both an internal and external witness of its authenticity. It had to be:

(1) **Apostolic** - written by an apostle or prophet or their associate
(2) **Orthodox** - universally conform to teachings of other apostles
(3) **Catholic** - accepted by the majority of churches
(4) **Self-authenticating** - demonstrate an edifying gospel power

---

Dear reader, you cannot know God personally and savingly without knowing him through his Word. John says as much in John 20:30-31: "*³⁰ Now Jesus did many other signs in the presence of the disciples, which are not written in this book; ³¹ but these are written so that you may believe that Jesus is the Christ, the Son of God, and that by believing you may have life in his name*" (emphasis mine).

The Scriptures point us to Christ, who perfectly kept God's Law on our behalf. And when we taste the Word's sweetness shown to us in Christ, and cultivate a growing appetite for his written Word, the more we come to look like the One whom this Book is about: the Living Word, Jesus Christ (John 1:1).

Our appetite for God's Word determines everything – it determines the degree to which we love Christ and look like him.

CHAPTER 1 DISCUSSION QUESTIONS

1. Fill out the "Bee Truthful Questionnaire" at the beginning of this chapter. Consider the most common obstacles that keep you from feeding consistently on the Word of God.

2. List some of the descriptions of God's Word in Psalm 19:7-18. In your small group, share which of your observations spoke to you the most? Why?

   7-11
   Inspire me

3. Have you ever been stung by our culture with respect to its views on the trustworthiness of the Bible?

4. Write out your own prayer asking the Holy Spirit to cultivate a hunger in your heart for the Word. Ask him for help in finding a path to overcome the obstacles that keep you from feeding consistently on the Scriptures.

T √
time - do other things
tired

FEAST WITH ME

Do you struggle with doubts concerning the trustworthiness of God's Word? Look up these verses to see what other claims Scripture makes about itself. If you're leading a group, print these verses on a separate sheet of paper or on strips to be read out loud by your small group. *Write it down — which one speaks to me & why?*

Proverbs 30:5

Matthew 4:4

John 17:17

1 Timothy 4:6

2 Timothy 3:16-17

1 Peter 1:23-25

CHAPTER 2

BEE-COMING A WOMAN
WHO CRAVES GOD'S WORD

For the first nine months of the twins' life, I nursed them. Until they got teeth. Then I tagged myself out due to the whole synchronized biting thing. But whether they were nursing or bottle-feeding, this truth rings true: every baby loves to be fed. For newborns, this is particularly true because they feed a lot, around every two hours, and I had two of them! In fact, the only thing I really remember for the first few months of their lives was that I sat on a navy blue couch nursing them – all day, every day.

My mother, who has since solved many of my twin conundrums, gave me the best gift I received from any of my baby showers. She gave me a twin Boppy® that was big enough to nurse them at the same time. It was an indescribable gift to finally get off that navy couch during the day! A twin nursing pillow is like a regular donut-shaped nursing pillow, but on steroids. It was a couple of feet square and sloped inward, which was genius because newborns can't support the weight of their heads.

So, this is how this would go. I'd put the first baby in a bouncer at the foot of the couch. Then, I'd take the second baby in one arm and the Boppy® in the other and sit down on the couch. Once the second baby was positioned, he would instantly start screaming because he knew what the nursing pillow and the couch meant, and he was demanding to know, why, if he was ready to eat, was the food not ready? "I mean; what kind of service is this?" Now, the first baby who is still in the bouncer would usually begin to cry, too, because, well, he was stuck in a bouncer and very likely felt like he was missing a meal. So, the routine was, both kids would be screaming their heads off. Then, I would pick up the first baby in the bouncer and put him on the Boppy® facing his brother to nurse. And you know what happened? Instantly the screaming stopped.

The twins were satisfied. They were hungry, craved milk, and were satisfied by it in a way that nothing else would do. Singing? Dumb idea. Peek-a-boo, forget about it. They wanted to eat! As the twins got older and more aware of their surroundings, they would smile at each other as they ate. And nursing became a really happy and sweet time because they were content that their cravings were being satisfied.

In chapter 1, we asked two questions. First, we asked "what is God's Word?" We discovered that God's Word is our spiritual food, and Psalm 19 makes some claims about the nature of that spiritual food: it is perfect, sure, right, pure, true, and righteous altogether.

The second question we asked was "can we believe those claims?" And Psalm 19 tells us that Gods' Word is indeed trustworthy. It is S.C.A.N. – sufficient, clear, authoritative, and necessary. God's Word is a good type of food for our souls, and in chapter 2, we're going to see that it is a satisfying kind of food. Only the Word of God can satisfy the deepest hunger pangs of our heart. God's Word satisfies us in the way that milk satisfies a newborn baby.

In 1 Peter 2:1-3, Peter says this: *"So put away all malice and all deceit and hypocrisy and envy and all slander.² Like newborn infants, long for the pure spiritual milk, that by it you may grow up into salvation— ³ if indeed you have tasted that the Lord is good"* (emphasis mine).

Peter is telling us that we should desire the Word of God in the same way that a newborn craves milk. We are to long for it, earnestly, ardently. We are to cry over it and look for it! But very often we don't crave God's Word with that intensity. We might know it's good, true, right, perfect, and believe it is trustworthy, but we don't agree that it is truly capable of satisfying us.

Too often, we go around looking to satisfy those hunger pangs of our hearts everywhere else before we go to God's Word. We go to our friends, Facebook, co-workers, families, best-selling authors, and even pastors before we go to the Creator of the Universe. We'll read every self-help book on the planet before going to *the* Book.

The same Barna study I quoted in chapter 1 reported that, increasingly, Bible readers (those who said they read the Bible at least every once in a while) only read the Bible when "they have a problem" they need solved or need direction (17 percent) or need comfort (15 percent). Among millennials (ages 18-29), 45 percent said they had no desire even to try to read the Bible more.[20]

In our church cultures, this is the overwhelming trend: we are desiring God's Word less for what it is, pure and right and perfect milk. We no longer crave God's Word because it satisfies our deepest need to have intimacy with God. When we do finally get hungry for the nourishment only it can provide, it seems we are coming to the table for all the wrong reasons.

TAKING A SPIRITUAL TASTE TEST

So, how does God's Word taste to you? Because your attitude toward how something tastes greatly influences your appetite for it. Our attitudes influence how often we eat a type of food and how much we eat it.

God's Word tastes bitter

While teaching this material during a women's discipleship weekend in Pittsburgh, I set up three brown paper bags on a table, and asked the ladies to take a spiritual taste test. I opened the first paper bag and pulled out a large bottle of cough syrup. To some women, God's Word tastes bitter when they read it, so they typically only read the Scriptures when they need some sort of relief. In fact, these women have to be on their death bed to open the Bible. They must really be feeling the effects of the sickness of their sin, and

God's Word becomes a last resort after trying everything else imaginable. While God's Word does, indeed, offer us comfort and a remedy for our problems, the problem with this palate is a woman won't see lasting change in her life. As soon as she begins to feel better, or her circumstances change, she will stop taking her medicine.

God's Word tastes bland

When I opened the second bag, I pulled out a bag of rice cakes. To some women, Scripture taste bland and boring, and, as a result, they will never cultivate an appetite for it. This woman reads the Bible only because she knows she's supposed to. She reads the Bible because it is the right thing to do for her spiritual health, but she doesn't particularly enjoy it.

I feel this way about kale. It promises to be the superfood of the decade, loaded with all sorts of vitamins and minerals, but honestly, I can't get past the taste. I might be able to choke down a few heavily-salted kale chips every once in a while, but because I don't appreciate its taste, I will never cultivate a craving to eat it every day.

You would be surprised how many women share this palate. As women ministering to women, we must be careful not to placate this palate by allowing Scripture to take a back seat in our women's ministries. We can't simply slip in a few Bible verses at our women's events and call them biblical or only offer Bible studies that make us feel good. This trend in women's discipleship is like trying to hide Kale in a fruit smoothie. It might make God's Word appear more palatable, but it will never produce lasting benefits in the lives of the women who ingest it, because as soon as she fulfills her duty, she will forget what she read. Not only will we produce biblically illiterate disciples, but we will rob disciples of the indescribable joy of learning to feast on God's Word for themselves.

God's Word tastes sweeter than honey

From the final paper bag in my spiritual taste test I pulled a giant bar of chocolate. The woman who believes that God's Word truly is sweeter than honey will delight in eating it, considering it a special treasure. She will crave it, search for it, and hide it away in her heart so she can savor its message and meaning in her life. This is the palate we want to cultivate – a heart that truly delights in God's Word so that even the seemingly difficult parts taste sweet because we've tasted the goodness of our Savior.

It was during that sugar-free diet that I told you about in the first chapter that I cultivated the little habit of hording chocolate in my kitchen cabinets. Like most mothers of young children, I have all manner of hiding places for my treats to keep them away from the grimy little hands that try to steal them. Now that the boys are almost as tall as I am, they can reach those nooks and crannies between the plates and mugs, so I've continually had to find new hiding places. I've had to go higher up and further back in my cabinets, going to greater lengths to keep my treasure private so I can savor it. The more we read God's Word, the more we will crave it, and the greater lengths we will go to savor its taste and benefits in our lives.

Among these palates, which do you most commonly have? Does Scripture taste bitter to you like cough syrup? Does it taste mostly bland as if you're munching on cardboard rice cakes? Or does the Word of God taste sweet to you? When we can honestly assess the state of our palate, we can move forward in cultivating an appetite for God's Word.

SPIRITUAL TASTE TEST

God's Word tastes like medicine
I read God's Word only when I'm feeling the effects of the sickness of my sin. When I read God's Word, it tastes bitter to me.

God's Word tastes like rice cakes
I read God's Word because it is the right thing to do for my health, but I don't particularly enjoy it. When I read God's Word, it tastes bland and boring.

God's Word tastes like chocolate
I read God's Word because I crave it. When I read God's Word, it tastes sweeter than honey.

So, let's look at what makes God's Word so sweet. Then maybe we can jumpstart our appetites for God's Word and change our eating habits in the process.

GOD'S WORD IS SWEETER THAN HONEY & GOLD

What makes God's Word sweet? Look at Psalm 19 again. Starting in verse 7, observe some of the ways God's Word is sweet. What does God's Word do *to* and *for* us? Let's call these effects our "sweet factors." Write them down in the discussion question space at the end of the chapter.

1. God's Word revives our soul.

In verse 7, the Psalmist says that God's Word "revives our souls." In the original language (Hebrew), the word revive means "to return." It is predominately used when the prophets called Israel to return to her God, but it also conveys the sense of a tired soul being refreshed or renewed. It paints the picture of a person being refreshed or restored to wholeness and soundness, which is interesting since the word for perfect means wholeness, soundness implying completeness. God's Word is sweet because it revives us.

2. God's Word makes us wise.

The rest of verse 7 says God's Word "makes wise the simple." I got a laugh recently when a preschool teacher I know posted something on Facebook she overheard in her classroom. One of her preschoolers observed, "I'm as smart as my brain lets me be." This is an incredibly profound statement for a preschooler, but it's also incredibly wrong! Our intelligence is, indeed, greatly influenced by our biology and genes, but

48

thankfully, we are more than our biology.

Contrary to popular science, we are not our brains. We are not, as many popular books testify, simply the sum of our biological parts.[21] Enlightenment thinkers of the 18-19th century quickly realized reason alone did not bring all the world's wisdom. What started as an optimistic worldview quickly dissolved into the pessimistic realization that mankind can know very little beyond the confines of the human senses. To know truth and love and all those things that cannot be measured or quantified by the scientific method, we need knowledge from an outside source – a source that stands outside the bounds of man's finite perceptions of the world. We have been given that source in the Word – God's revelation about himself and about the world. And most importantly, it is through God's written Word that we can come to know true Wisdom, the Living Word, Jesus Christ, himself.

God's Word is sweet because it gives us wisdom we can obtain by no other means.

3. God's Word makes us joyful.

In verse 8, we see that God's Word is sweet not just because it restores us and makes us wise, but also because it gives us joy. The joy found in the Word speaks to more than simply happy feelings that come and go based on circumstances, but an internal condition of "inner peace and tranquility" (Ps. 119:165; Is. 26:3; John 16:33). This type of joy or inner peace is not to be viewed as the cherry on top of a salvation sundae, another blessing from our good God. Our joy stems from a right relationship with God, being returned to him.[22] This joy is eternal because its source is eternal. Just as divine wisdom confounds the world, so does divine joy. The world cannot comprehend the cancer patient who sings her Creator's praises in the midst of her suffering, nor the mother who testifies to her God's grace at the loss of a child.

God's Word is sweet because it brings us joy.

4. God's Word enlightens our eyes.

Verse 8 also says God's Word "enlightens our eyes." It helps us see clearly and without distortion or darkness. In the same way that prescription glasses bring our surroundings into focus, God's Word helps us view life as he views it. With his perspective through which to filter our world, we can perceive sin as sin and truth as truth (Heb. 4:11-13). Without such a clear view, we could never correctly assess our need for help, hope to find our way back to God on our own, much less possess wisdom or joy for the journey. Our eyes need enlightening to see the depth of our sin rather than excuse it, mitigate it, or blame others.

So, God's Word is sweet because it helps us to see and interpret life correctly. Whoever said, "the eyes are the window to the soul," accurately, however unwittingly, described the eyes of a new believer. If you have ever seen the face of a woman who has been recently changed by the Word of God, you will agree that it is a beautiful sight to behold. I've seen the countenance of sullen and dark teenagers transform overnight into the faces of young women luminous with joy. I've seen timid and hopeless women become bold and purposeful as the change that began inside of them becomes proportionately reflected on the outside. It is one reason why I'm passionate about discipling new believers, particularly those who have never tasted the Scriptures before. My joy and attitude for the Bible increases as I watch them take delight in devouring the Word of our Lord. Attitude is catching. If you want to grow in your appetite for God's Word, simply disciple a new believer and watch their joy in the Word become yours.

At this point, I want to stop and ask you to observe something about these effects we've noted and their progression. Look at where the author begins in verse 7. He begins with the innermost part of our personal identity, our soul. Next, the Psalmist moves to our mind. Then, he speaks of our heart, and lastly, our eyes (body). The Word of God touches our soul, mind, heart, body. The author could be making a point: *God's Word is beneficial for every part of us*. It is not just important to read the Bible so we can know God or know about him. Bible study and application is the means by which our entire being is transformed to look and live like him. This is the natural shape of discipleship.[23] When we come to salvation, we are first converted in our souls (restored to God), then we are made wise through the knowledge of Christ (renewed in our minds). Next, we are made glad in our hearts, and lastly, we are given eyes to see and perceive truth and service rightly.

Ultimately, the result of this progression of discipleship appears in verse 9: we fear the Lord. We no longer fear the world. We are no longer driven by worldly appetites, but rather, we begin to hunger for God's truth. We are transformed from the inside out by an outside force – God's Word. And this transformation brings lasting change. God's Word is sweet for all these reasons – it restores us, makes us wise, glad, and helps us see clearly. It transforms us, and this transformation involves the total person, which leads the Psalmist to this central conclusion in verse 10 concerning the Scriptures: *"More are they to be desired than gold, even much fine gold. Sweeter also than honey, and drippings of the honeycomb."*

God's Word offers us what honey and gold cannot. That's saying a lot because in the historical context of Psalm 19, if you had honey and gold, you were set for life.

The benefits of honey and gold

Consider some of the ways honey is used today and add its benefits to notes at the end of the chapter. Both bee pollen and raw honey are commonly used as homeopathic remedies to promote overall well-being and health. Because it contains antimicrobial agents and antioxidants, some call honey "liquid gold." Along with medicinal purposes, honey is also used as a natural sweetener. And for some brave souls, keeping bees offers a satisfying way to generate a substantive income. Generally speaking, honey provides some generous benefits: income, satisfaction, good health, and general well-being.

What about the benefits of gold? Its benefits are more obvious. In a day when the value of paper currency constantly fluctuates, having gold can instantly make you rich. For centuries, gold was the basis for currency and commerce. Governments produced coins and paper monies and determined their value based on gold reserves, giving us the phrase "gold standard" - a phrase referring to reliability and prestige. Just as gold brings wealth to the one who owns it, it can similarly yield great power. What was true in ancient cultures still rings true today: the one who "controls the purse" controls the fate of homes, corporations, entities, and even nations.

Today, women are becoming increasingly independently wealthy, more so through corporate employment and investments than through the traditional venues of marriage or inheritance. This new-found independence makes heavy promises for the pursuit of happiness, particularly for women seeking financial and physical security.

Our independence comes not just in how we gain our wealth, but also in how we choose to use it. If you're anything like the average woman, you'll unload a small fortune on the latest anti-aging creams and beauty products based on the promise of an improved appearance. In 2013, *InStyle* magazine estimated that women spend upwards of $15,000 on beauty products in their lifetime. Using data collected by the savings tool Mint.com, the same *InStyle* report indicated a woman will spend $3,770 on mascara, $2,750 on eye shadow, and $1,780 on lipstick![24] Anti-aging products represent a multibillion-dollar industry, about $261.9 billion in 2013.[25] Beauty is a lucrative pursuit for many companies, mainly because it is a bottomless pursuit for many women.

Gold, then, can be used to make ourselves rich, powerful, pretty, and safe. Those benefits are nothing to sniff at. In fact, much of the world spends most of their time pursing one or more of those goals.

But, can gold and honey give you any of the same benefits that God's Word provides? I think you could make the case for some! You could spend all your gold on books, yet still miss knowing the source of all truth. You can use honey to enhance your appearance, but beauty only goes skin deep. You could purchase the best security-system in the world, but not even the best security detail can promise eternal bliss.

The benefits of honey and gold are temporal; they cease when the honey and gold dry up. We cannot enjoy their derivatives in death, and they are less likely to be enjoyed in tragedy. Only those benefits that come from the sweetness of God's Word endure despite darkness, death, tragedy, and loss. Only the change that comes from the transformation of the total person - soul, mind, heart, body - through the Word "endures forever."

God's Word has life-altering, life-giving effects that are unfading and unending. When we taste God's Word, we are forever marked and changed by it. But here's the key to our search for happiness: *we are only changed by God's Word to the degree that we feed on it.*

BEE-COMING WOMEN OF THE WORD

Our cravings drive our appetites. If we crave God's Word, we will feed on it consistently and enjoy the blessings of transformation that come from it. However, if we crave other things more than God's Word - being noticed, being good, being right, being safe, being applauded - then our diet will consist of other things. We will consume beauty products, new clothes, full schedules or no schedules, to-do lists, information.

Oh, we might enjoy God's Word every once in a while, such as when we attend a retreat or go to church on Sunday morning, like a piece of cake on a special occasion. We might treat God's Word like that go-to granola bar when we need a quick fix to our heart's hunger pangs – to be encouraged, find direction, or feel loved. If we do not crave God's Word consistently, we won't feed on it consistently. Our cravings drive our appetites. We will only consume what we truly desire.

So, at this point I want to ask each of you: do you crave God's Word? You know the answer to this question already, deep down. Do you crave to know God through his Word more than anything else? Because you are either a woman who craves the *world* or a woman who craves the *Word*. These are two very different women with two very different destinies.

A *woman who craves the world* is one who is overcome and undone in her constant search for pleasure, satisfaction, good health, and well-being. She seeks satisfaction from temporal realities provided by the things of this world, including wealth, health, power, beauty, and safety. None of these are bad things in and of themselves – wealth, health, power, beauty, and security. But a woman of the world foolishly pursues those things that do not provide lasting effects to the exclusion of all in her life. What she pursues will eventually control her (John 8:34, Rom. 6:20).

But only a woman who craves the Word of God above all else can be called a woman of the Word. A *woman of the Word* is one who is overcome and secure in her consistent study of the Scriptures. She seeks the eternal realities offered through the Word of God and is set free to dwell in the righteousness of Christ (2 Cor. 5:14-21; Gal. 5:5).

A woman who craves the Word has submitted her whole self to God's Word. Such women dot the pages of Scripture. Ruth chose to trust in the God of Israel over the gods of her hometown in the midst of terrifying loss (Ruth 1:16-17). Mary, the mother of Jesus, chose to cling to the promises of God in the face of sure poverty and marginalization had her husband chosen to divorce her (Luke 1:46-55). For many of us, those stories seem irrelevant for modern life, offering impossibly high standards and crushing burdens. Thankfully, Psalm 19 fills in some of the details of what a woman of the Word looks like and how she cultivates her appetite for it above all else. A woman who craves the Word displays two key markers according to this song.

Women of the Word submit to its authority (Ps. 19:8-10)

More than a checklist for holiness or a list of DOs and DON'Ts, a woman of the Word trusts that God's Word offers her the right way to live. In verse 8, we learned that "*the precepts of the Lord are right, rejoicing the heart;*" meaning God's Word says right things, righteous things. A woman who craves the Word submits to the authority of God's Word trusting that its principles are right.

But a woman of the Word not only trusts that the Word offers her the right way to live, she also trusts that it offers her the *best* way to live. Right and best:

the two don't always seem the same.

We can agree that a course of action is "right," but we might disagree that it is actually the "best" thing to do. I have this discussion on what seems like a daily basis with the twins. In their 8-year-old brains, they might be able to understand a little why it is right to share, love, and build up one another – because the Bible tells them so, because Mom requires it, and because Christ shared himself with them. But, they certainly won't be happy about having to share, love, and build up one another, especially when there is no payoff in the end or reward in sight. One brother can see how sharing Legos® benefits the other brother, but most of the time he is left to wonder how giving away his Legos® benefits him.

As women, we do the same thing. Refusing to be self-promoting and demanding in the office might be the right thing to do in order to embrace the mind of Christ, but how is that best when that new job opening might go to someone else who isn't afraid to toot their own horn? A mom who devotes her life to serving her family might know that her selfless acts of service are right and good for her household, but when she crawls into bed each night feeling like she's been hit by a mack truck, repeatedly, she might wonder if the decision to serve others is truly best for her. In each of those illustrations, there is balance to be had, but generally speaking, a woman who craves God's Word submits to the authority of God's Word trusting it's the best way to live because it says both right things and it says right things *for her.*

That means she won't grumble when she gets to those passages which prove to be so unsavory to our culture milieu – passages on sacrifice, sexuality, service, submission. Instead her submission to the authority of the Word in those matters that seem distasteful will be marked by joy, strength, and peaceful perseverance.

Now, listen ya'll. I'm not trying to Proverbs-31 you. I'm not trying to guilt you into striving to become the perfect woman next door who appears to wield ninja skills in successfully balancing her family, work, home, and church life. I'm not trying to squeeze you into an Instagram picture of that size-two designer friend whose family looks like they just stepped out of a Banana Republic ad with #nofilter.

Nor am I trying to make you feel like you'll never arrive at becoming a woman of the Word until you put to death all those competing cravings. Because no matter how much some of us seem to have it all together, none of us does. No one measures up against the standard of Christ revealed in the Word. But here's the soul-relieving news. Psalm 19 reveals that a woman of the Word is not an *impossible standard*, but rather, a *posture of the heart*. Submission is not really about what we do, but the stance our heart takes toward life as God has orchestrated it and toward those we love. Are we willingly stepping under the leadership of our Lord to do what is right and trusting it is best, or are we bowing up inside? Do we live our lives like we believe God knows what will truly benefit us, or do we think we can sort out our affairs and manage our destiny on our own?

A woman of the Word is a woman who, after tasting the sweetness of her Savior, makes room in her heart for the Spirit to grow true joy, especially when she comes to those parts of her spiritual meal that appear bitter at first. And because of the Spirit's work in her life, she truly enjoys eating them, and that isn't because she's ignorant or naïve or a victim of patriarchal religion (all those insults our culture hurls at us). She enjoys the principles and precepts of God's Word because of the Spirit's work in her life helping her to trust that they are the best way to live.

A woman who craves God's Word has a spiritual appetite first built upon what happened to her soul and mind in verses 7-8. It revived her soul and made her wise in Christ.

Women of the Word submit to its correction (Ps. 19:11-14)

But not only does a woman of the Word submit to the Word's *authority*, the Psalmist says a woman of the Word also submits to its *correction*. I am so glad the Psalmist added these final verses to this chapter. They are crucial for us to get the full picture of God's purposes in revealing himself to us and how we can become women who crave his Word, otherwise we might be tempted to discouragement.

The Psalmist reminds us that God's revelation is always tied up with his redemption. Always! And when we become women of the Word, we become women in whom God is working out his mighty redemptive purposes. He is at work in our lives to make us look like him. In doing so, a woman of the Word submits to the Bible's correction. And she does this, according to our passage, in two ways: by allowing it to *keep* her from sin and to *cleanse* her from sin.

God's Word keeps her from sin

Verse 11 says, *"Moreover, by them is your servant warned; in keeping them there is great reward."* Notice the word "servant" used here; a woman of the Word takes the posture of Christ, a servant. But more specifically, this is how God's Word is at work in her: when a woman craves God's Word more than the world, she will find that she is kept from sin. She is kept from the snares of life that easily entangle her (Heb. 12:1-2). God's Word acts as a warning to us, ladies. If God tells us what is right and best in his Word, he is equally clear about what is evil and what would be disastrous for us.

If we have hidden God's Word in our hearts and willingly submit to its correction, then we will be warned when we are tempted to indulge in those old cravings. Look at the rest of verse 11. It reads, *"and in keeping them there is great reward."* There is a reward in keeping God's Word. What kind of reward do you think we receive when we submit to the correction of the Word? Blessings? Safety? Security? Prosperity? While "reward" could refer to any number of the natural consequences that play out in our lives when we choose right and righteousness, I think the Psalmist is referring to one specific reward.

Whenever I read the word "reward" in the Bible, I am instantly transported to the story of Abram. In Gen. 15:1, God is consoling Abram that his promise to him was indeed trustworthy. God promised to make Abram the father of many nations. And when Abram, who was over 100 years old at this point, expressed wonder at such a promise, God said, *"Do not be afraid, Abram, I am your Shield, your exceedingly great reward."*

God meant this: "I am your reward, not the blessings I give you, not the possessions I allow you to steward, nor the title of Father of the Nations that I've promised you. Just me. I'm your reward. Oh, and Abram, I am your Shield, too. I am keeping you in me. I'm shielding you in this covenant relationship so I can make you mine. I am your reward and you are mine!"

This might sound counter-intuitive because in our culture, rewards often come about by works of our own hand. We win awards, earn raises, score points – all by our own efforts. But, in Christ, "reward" whispers to who he is and what he does. In the Bible, reward is about a relationship with Christ, who is our ultimate reward.

Ladies, there is great reward in craving and keeping God's Word, not because God is blessing the work of our hands, but because he is blessing his work in us – the result of the Word in our lives. God's Word keeps us from sin by keeping us in him, our exceedingly great reward. This isn't, "Hey, if you keep every one of my commands, I'll reward you." Nor is it, "Here's another sticker for your good behavior chart!" Rather, God is saying, "When you willingly submit to my authority, the natural consequence is you will be protected and kept in me. I am going to shield you and keep you in me so we are each other's reward" (Eph. 1:18-19).

God's Word cleanses her from sin

So, a woman of the Word submits to the Bible's correction, allowing it to *keep* her from sin, but she also allows it to *cleanse* her from sin. Re-read verses 12-13: *"Who can discern his errors? Declare me innocent from hid-*

den faults. ¹³ Keep back your servant also from presumptuous sins; let them not have dominion over me! Then I shall be blameless, and innocent of great transgression."

We cannot discern all our own errors, the Psalmist says. Our eyes are enlightened by God's Word, but we don't yet have 20/20 vision. One day we will because we will look like Christ, and we will finally be able to "see" him as he is (1 John 3:2). But until that day, we will always need help seeing the depths of our own darkness. That's why the Psalmist says, *"Declare me innocent from hidden faults. ¹³ Keep back your servant also from presumptuous sins; let them not have dominion over me!"*

In his commentary on Psalm 19, British scholar and author John Phillips uses some helpful terms to distinguish what's going on in this passage. He uses the terms *radical* cleansing versus *recurrent* cleansing.[26] In Jesus, Phillips says, we are radically cleansed from sin. All our sins in the past, present, and future are forgiven in him. But despite being forgiven, we still continue to sin. We are still sinners. However, here's the difference. After we've been restored to a right relationship to the Father through the Son, any new sin we commit doesn't change our standing before God as redeemed. Even as sin inevitably damages our relationship with him and others around us, it cannot change our position before him.

In the Old Testament, you get a clear picture of this truth with a specific instrument God commanded to be put in the Temple – the laver. The laver was a bronze basin or bowl filled with water. It was located in the court of priests, between the steps that lead up into the Holy of Holies and the altar of burnt offering, where the people sacrificed animals to show God they were trusting in the price he paid for their salvation. This laver was used by the priests to wash themselves, not just their hands, but their feet, too.

Interestingly, it was constructed from the bronze mirrors of the women so that when one came face to face with the laver, they saw not just water, but their own reflection, a sinner. The laver "both revealed and removed defilement," symbolizing the cleansing function of God's Word.[27] God's Word cleanses us, and it does so by revealing to us areas of sin in our lives.

This is the message of Psalm 19: we are changed by God's Word in a progressive manner to look more like him. God's Word revives our souls, makes us wise, makes us glad, and makes us lovely. We are changed in spirit, mind, heart, and body. God's Word is the laver of our soul, revealing recurrent sin and cleansing us from within, and the result is we are being transformed to look holy like Christ.

So, does that mean we are perfect? That little phrase, *"Then I shall be blameless And I shall be innocent of great transgression"* in verse 13 is important. Innocent means, literally, "to be cleaned, be free from guilt, to be free from obligation."[28] The NASB version translates verse 13, *"I shall be acquitted of great transgression"* (emphasis mine). To be declared not guilty doesn't mean we actually are not guilty. We have, as the NASB helps us see, been acquitted. A provision has been put in place or in effect in our lives that changes our standing before the Law Giver. Who puts that change into effect? The Redeemer, who is the Word (John 1:1). Verse 14 says, *"Let the words of my mouth and the meditation of my heart Be acceptable in Your sight, O Lord, my strength and my Redeemer."*

Christ, the Living, Spoken Word, stands over us, not as an accuser of what we have done wrong or how we have failed to read his Word every day. He stands over us as a Refuge and Shield (Prov. 14:26). One of his means of protection is his written Word where we get to come to him personally, and enjoy change and transformation that is caused by him, so we can look like him and sound like him and have a heart like his.

A woman who craves the Word submits to the Word's authority and correction. She is a woman who desires her Redeemer above all, and he is her *"Shield and exceedingly great reward"* (Gen. 15:1).

CULTIVATING AN APPETITE FOR GOD'S WORD

One note of application here: we must first be changed by the Living Word in order to crave his written Word. Our attitude for God's Word precedes appetite. You might be thinking, "I am trying to read the Bible, but I just don't get it! It's boring." Or you might be wondering, "Why don't I think Scripture tastes sweet? Why are its teachings so hard to swallow?"

I would ask you to take another spiritual taste test and ask yourself, "Do I really think the Savior is sweet?" Because our attitude toward God's Son will always determine the size of our appetite for God's Word. Do I truly rejoice in my Savior and what he has done for me? Have I been changed by Christ first? It starts with our attitude. Our attitude impacts our appetite. But then, as Bible study teacher Howard Hendricks points out, our appetite impacts the aim of the

Scriptures in our life.[29]

The aim of God's Word is to change us! We aren't to read the Bible just to make us better women, to sin less and do more good, or to be better versions of ourselves, or even to empower us to reach our potential. The goal of God's Word is to make us whole, complete in Christ (Heb. 5:1-12; Col. 2:10; 2 Tim. 3:16-17). By the end of our lives, we are to look more like Christ – who lived the perfect life on earth we were created to enjoy. Reading the Scriptures, immersing ourselves in them, delighting in them, makes us look more like Christ and more like the humans we were intended to be when God first created mankind. This is not a process of change we control, but one we participate in through the Spirit's work (Heb. 13:20-21).

Attitude → Appetite → Aim

When we crave something, we eat it, and it impacts the way we look. I have to honest. I have a pretty big sweet tooth (and carb tooth), so I am prone to eating sweet foods, and if I'm not careful, they can easily impact my health for better or worse. My attitude toward a type of food impacts my appetite for it, and my appetite for a food will impact the end result of my diet and physical health. Attitude → Appetite → Aim.

But there is something else you should know: our appetites can be cyclical. The more our body is impacted by a type of food we eat, the more we will crave it. The more I rely on coffee to wake myself up in the morning, the more my body will require it for energy. Even if you're not a coffee person, think about how easy food addictions can commandeer our diet and our lives.

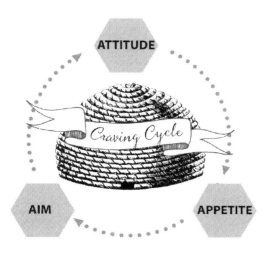

Spiritually speaking, the cyclical nature of the craving cycle explains many of the challenges we face when trying to cultivate a consistent appetite for God's Word. When we stop reading God's Word (appetite), we stop looking like Christ because the process of sanctification slows down (aim). When we are no longer being changed by God's Word, we crave it less (attitude). And the less we crave it, the less we actually study it (appetite). And so forth.

You might want to become a woman of the Word, but don't know where to begin. You need help knowing where to jump into God's Word. Or, you might have realized that you were once setting the pace in God's Word, but somewhere along your journey you got off track, and now you are having trouble jumping back in.

Spend some time in your small group or individually to evaluate your own appetite for God's Word, identifying any parts of the cycle where you tend to get stuck. Consider some ways you can cultivate an appetite for God's Word listed at the end of this chapter, and share your own ideas for how you can increase your spiritual cravings for God's Word.

CONCLUSION

If you've never tasted that the Lord is good, I invite you to do so right now. Our sweet Savior has saved a seat at his table with your name on it so you can taste for yourself his sweetness. He stands ready to transform you into his very image and help you become a woman of his Word, the woman he created you to be – refreshed, wise, joyful, and purposeful.

So far, we've talked about what God's Word is and why it is a trustworthy source for knowledge on how to live the best possible life. We've also discussed what women look like who trust in God's Word above all else. In the next chapter, we'll talk about *how* you can "bee-come" a woman of the Word with some practical tools for reading, studying, and applying God's Word.

God's Word is spiritual food.

3 BAD EATING HABITS

Bad Eating Habit #1: Horking it Down

In the animated film, *Ratatouille*, Remy the rat screams to his brother: "No, don't hork it down. Chew it slowly, and only think about the taste." God's Word is not a means to an end. We do not hork it down out of duty or because it's a necessity to spiritual growth. To cultivate our appetite we must savor the words, digest their meaning, and see the fruit that it produces through the Spirit.

Bad Eating Habit #2: Picking Around

Left to her own palate, the Picky Eater will only ingest the foods she likes from God's Word, rather than dining on its whole counsel. She removes herself from the natural rhythm of feeding on God's Word (attitude > appetite > aim), and as a result she does not enjoy the lasting fruit produced by consistent study of the Scriptures.

Bad Eating Habit #3: Food Snobbery

The Food Snob prides herself on dining on the "most important" or doctrinally-rich portions of Scripture. She would rather argue about how Scripture tastes (interpreting Scripture), rather than do the hard work of digesting it (applying Scripture). She is prone to looking down on others who don't share her eating habits.

3 Foods that Curb Our Cravings for God's Word

 ## Toxic Food

Toxic foods are sinful foods. Peter lists a few in 1 Pet. 2:1-3 (malice, deceit, hypocrisy, envy, and slander). These dangerous foods may taste sweet at first, but they will poison the soul. The more our spiritual appetites are driven by unhealthy cravings, the unhealthier our appetites become.

 ## Junk Food

Junk foods are spiritually-shallow resources, prepared by others. Instead of choosing foods that are easy to eat and digest, Peter says we should long for the "pure spiritual milk" of the Word that helps grow our appetites toward solid foods (1 Pet. 2:1-3; Heb. 5:12).

 ## Fast Food

Fast food is for a woman who is so busy she skips meals and grabs snacks on-the-go. If we are too busy serving God's church to refuel on God's Word, we will eventually run out of gas. The less we ingest of God's Word, the less we will desire it.

CHAPTER 2 DISCUSSION QUESTIONS

1. How does God's Word tastes to you - bitter, bland, or (sweet?) How has your palate for God's Word impacted the way you feed on it?

   Within a month of being saved, I began tasting the goodness of God - lost job, led Grandma to Lord, immersed, discipled 2 yrs.

2. List the "sweet factors" of God's Word found in Psalm 19:7-14. Next, list some benefits of gold and honey. How do they compare?

   perfect, sure, right, pure clean, true

3. *pg 64* What is curbing your spiritual appetite for the Word? Why do you crave it and what has been the result in your life?

   no curbing

   It's a safe place for me. # keeps changing me Exciting. God daily does thing to show me He loves me — insurance cards

4. Prayerfully examine your attitude toward God's Word and ask the Spirit to cultivate an appetite for God's Word in your heart. Write out a prayer.

FEAST WITH ME

Familiarize your small group with their Bible. Point out these important parts, where they are located, and how to use them: table of contents, the indexes, and the Old and New Testaments.[30]

Old Testament:
Law (Genesis – Deuteronomy)
History (Joshua – Esther)
Poetry & Wisdom (Job – Song of Solomon)
Major Prophets (Isaiah – Daniel)
Minor Prophets (Hosea – Malachi)

New Testament:
Gospels (Matthew – John)
History (Acts)
Letters/Epistles (1 Corinthians – Revelation)

PART II:

Feasting on the Word of God

CHAPTER 3

OBSERVATION? WHAT DO
I SEE?

God's Word is key to our spiritual nourishment and growth. He has designed us in such a way that the more we feed on his Word, the more our appetites and cravings for it will grow. That's because the more we eat it, the more we experience its good benefits. Psalm 19 tells us some of these benefits include life, wisdom, and joy. In this chapter, I want to share some practical strategies for increasing your spiritual appetite. If the previous two chapters were the feast, chapter 3 will give us a hands-on cooking lesson.

Think of a chef and the care he or she takes in understanding and prepping the ingredients for a dish, carefully cooking it, and then plating it in a beautiful way. It doesn't matter how many cooking shows I watch on the Food Network or how many great chefs I observe at work, if I want to eat and eat in a healthy way, I will eventually have to learn to cook for myself.

The same applies to studying God's Word. It

doesn't matter how many Bible studies I attend or how many great teachers I sit under as they prepare a meal for me out of God's Word, If I'm not making my own discoveries, I will never get excited about how the Word of God tastes. I will never understand the joy of preparing a meal from his Word for myself. Getting excited about getting in the kitchen will keep God's Word from tasting like rice cakes! So, in order to cultivate a growing appetite for God's Word, a student must be able to make discoveries for herself. We call this self-feeding.

In retrospect, I think Bible study became exciting for me when it became personal - when I learned how to mine the depths of Scripture for myself. Despite growing up in a Bible-honoring home and attending church throughout my childhood, it wasn't until I was in my late 20s that I actually learned how to feed on the Scriptures for myself. Until that point, I relied on the teachings served up by other capable cooks like my pastors, popular authors, and my parents.

For me, this was the key: when I began to study the Bible for myself, making my own discoveries, I truly fell in love with the Scriptures.[31] Today, I truly know them to be sweeter than honey. It began when the Word of God became very personal to me, but that didn't happen by accident. Cultivating an appetite for God's Word will only happen if you intentionally commit yourself to studying it.

Bee-ing Truthful

In chapter one, I asked each of you to "bee truthful" and evaluate how often you read the Bible and what keeps you from reading the Bible. When I pose these questions to Bible study friends or my online community, the results are usually strikingly similar. Most often, women say they are too busy to feed on God's Word consistently. I battle this obstacle, too. Between work, church service, family needs, special projects, and everyday life in general, Bible study can easily fall to the bottom of my survival list. Others commonly tell me that God's Word seems confusing to them. It is hard to cultivate an appetite for something if you don't understand how to eat it or even what you're eating.

In this chapter, we will unlock a simple strategy for studying and applying God's Word that will help remove some of those obstacles. I love the Bible study method I am presenting to you for three reasons:

First, it works! This is the method of Bible study I use. I learned it in seminary and have continued to use it since. It has helped me grow leaps and bounds in understanding not just what God's Word says, but who God is.

Second, it grows! You can add layers to this Bible study method, causing your knowledge and love to deepen as you dig deeper into the Scriptures.

Third, it's for everybody! This method is for all believers of any level of spiritual maturity. A new believer with no Bible background can use this method just as easily as someone who has been studying the Bible for years. This method is for everybody.

So, what is this method? It is the OIA method outlined by Howard Hendricks in *Living by the Book.* If you don't have this book, buy it now. Get on your amazon app and purchase it, because it will change how you read, study, and apply God's Word. It will give you the tools to self-feed, to look at the parts and prepare a substantial meal on which to feast. My book differs in that I offer a more concise version of this process specifically for first-time Bible students, adding insights for women who feel led to teach others how to study God's Word.

The OIA Model has three steps, which we will break apart in the next three chapters: observation, interpretation, and application. Those are Hendricks' terms. They are straightforward but sort of technical, too. Each part of this method asks a question.

What do I see?
OBSERVATION

What does it say?
INTERPRETATION

What do I do?
APPLICATION

First, **observation asks, *"What do I see?"*** In this first phase of Bible study, think of yourself as an investigator. You are using a magnifying glass to look for the details and facts presented by the text.

Second, **interpretation asks, *"What does it say?"*** In this phase, think of yourself as a translator. You are translating the meaning of a message to someone else. You are taking those facts you observed and interpreting what they mean.

Third, **application asks, *"What do I do?"*** In the final phase of Bible study, think of yourself as an engineer. You are putting all the pieces to work in your life, with the Spirit's help, in a meaningful way.

Hendricks uses the bigger terms: observation, interpretation, application. But if you are new to studying the Bible, you can remember the three steps this way: see, say, and do.

Don't be scared of the size of these words, however, because if you've read chapters 1 and 2, you've already used this method! First, we made some observations about God's Word from Psalm 19. Remember, we used our magnifying glass to discover the claims Psalm 19 made about God's Word. (We discovered it is perfect, right, true, and more). Then, we interpreted those facts about God's Word to mean that God's Word is trustworthy. Finally, we applied the message, putting it to work in our lives noting we must become women who crave God's Word by submitting to its authority and correction.

So, you've already used this three-part method of observation, interpretation, application (see, say, do) to feast on Psalm 19. You did it, and you can do this now! So, let's start with observation, and then I want you to spend some of your own time in the kitchen.

OBSERVATION: WHAT DO I SEE?

 My biggest pet peeve is something I call Bible study whiplash. Oh, it's real, and it is painful! It can even be deadly! Bible study whiplash is this: someone reads a verse or passage, and then the first thing they ask is, "What does that mean to you?"

When I hear this question asked in a Sunday School class or a small group, I want to scream. (Although I usually just close my Bible and start making my grocery list). To me, that question feels like getting hit from behind by a moving vehicle. It's not that it is an irrelevant question, but it's not the first question we should be asking when we read a Bible passage. It's not even the second question! It's actually the last question we should ask!

The person who asks, "What does that mean to you?" is what I call a negligent reader, sort of like a negligent driver. She is plodding down the road, completely oblivious to what's going on around her. She's probably doing ten other things: putting on her mascara, eating breakfast, yelling at the kids, texting. She is completely missing all the signals the author has purposefully put in the passage to try to get her attention. She plows through every stop sign in the text, speeds the whole way, and then screeches to a halt when she gets to her destination – the application part of her Bible study. Talk about horking it down! Ladies, do not be this kind of Bible study lady. Do not be Whiplash Wilma! Because like her name suggests, Whiplash Wilma can do real damage to herself and others as a negligent student of God's Word.

When you are driving through Scripture, you must look for signs the author intentionally put there. This is the part of our Bible study method called observation. It is the most important part of the Bible study process because how well you observe what's in a passage determines how well you are able to interpret it and apply it to your life.

An Experiment

I'm convinced that too often we are negligent readers because we really don't know how to observe facts. So, let's have some fun. Grab a No. 2 pencil and a timer. In just three minutes, write down as many observations as you can about that pencil in the box at the end of the chapter. Consider what it looks like, how to describe it, and/or what it does.

How many observations did you make? 5? 10? 15? 20? 25? If you are doing this experiment in a group, compare your observations.

So, here's the deal. Author Howard Hendricks was a Dallas Theological Seminary professor. My friend enrolled in his class on this very subject. As homework, he sent the class home with a pencil and asked them to make 100 observations about it. They came to class, shared their observations, and then, to my friend's horror, he sent them home to repeat the assignment all over again. He wanted 100 new observations.

You might be thinking, gosh, that sounds like a lot of work! But Howard Hendricks, a veteran Bible study teacher, knew that if you don't spend adequate time observing what is in the text, you can easily miss what the author was really trying to communicate. When we are tempted to rush through a passage, we end up making it all about us. That's not self-feeding; that's called horking it down. Not only will you choke in the process, you'll miss out on experiencing the true flavor of the text.

So, we must do the hard work of "seeing" what's really there. Let me encourage you. If you do the hard work of observation – and really do it justice – two things will happen:

First, *it gets easier the more you practice*. Once you train your eye to look for details, details will begin to fly out at you, and you will discover that minor details are not minor at all.

And second, the more time you spend in observation *the less work you will have to do in other parts of the method*. As Hendricks points out in his book, the more time you spending outlining "what you see" the less time you'll have to spend in trying to determine what a passage has to "say" and what it compels you to "do" in response.[32] So, when you read a passage with your magnifying glass, what are you supposed to look for?

LOOKING FOR CLUES

Five "W" Questions

In any text, look for answers to the five "W" questions: who, what, when, where, and why. My undergraduate degree is in journalism, and in my very first journalism class we were taught to ask the five "W" questions during interviews and then cram all the answers in the lead paragraph of a news story. Why? Getting all the key facts up front in a news story gives clarity to the article.

In observing a text, ask yourself these five "W" questions:

Who: who is talking? Who is the author talking to? Who is he talking about? Who are the main characters?

What: what is happening in this passage? What is

the author saying?

When: when is this passage taking place? Is the speaker talking about a time when something is going to take place? When was the book or letter written?

Where: what is the geographic location of the writer and reader? What's going on there? Does the speaker refer to another place?

Why: why is the author writing? Why is the speaker sharing his message? Why is an event happening? Is there a reason for a story? The 'why' and 'how' are sometimes easier to discern in some parts of Scriptures. For instance, in the letters of the New Testament, the authors will clearly reveal their intentions, saying something like, "I'm writing to you because of false teachers among you" (2 Pet. 2:1-3; 1 John 4:1; Titus 1:11; 1 Tim. 6:3-5).

So, when you read a passage, ask those five "W" questions of the text: who, what, when, where, and why. As a new Bible study student, don't get discouraged if you can't discern all these facts at first. I've found that reading a passage once through without stopping helps. Next, I write out these five "W" words on a separate sheet of paper and fill them in as I read the passage for a second time. Writing them out by hand helps me keep all the facts straight. In fact, when I write a lead paragraph for a news article, I still write out these five key words and fill them in so my article has greater clarity. But beyond the five "W" questions, there are other things to look for.

Key Words

Look for key words in the text, words that seem

important to the writer. Here's just two examples. In the Old Testament, we see specific titles used of God. Those aren't just names used to identify an individual like Bob or Greg; the biblical writers employs a specific name for God for a specific reason.[33] Descriptors like rock and refuge (Ps. 18:2) or titles such as Lord of Hosts (1 Sam. 1:3) are used as a way to teach us about the nature, character, and activity of God.

In the New Testament, the apostle Paul uses key words pertaining to doctrine. You'll see words such as redemption, salvation, sanctification. Those are key words that you should note and spend some time investigating further. Don't let key words pass by without stopping to observe them.

Repeated Words

Look for repeated words in a passage. If an author is repeating something, he is trying to emphasize something. So, we'd better pay attention. Those repeated words or repeated themes are very likely pushing us toward a main point.

Tense of Words

Look for the tense of word an author uses. Verb tenses reveal a lot about an action, including the significance or the scope of an action. If it's been a while since you were seated in English class, you might want to brush up on your verb mood and tenses, parts of speech, or other sentence components.[34]

For first-time Bible students, start by observing these terms and how they appear in the English. Note the number of times they appear in the passage. When you see them, underline them or write them down on a separate piece of paper. You can look them up later in a Bible dictionary or take them to your discipleship leader and work through them together.

For disciplers, be sure to have a good handle on key doctrinal terms used in the Scriptures, what they mean and the way they are being used in a passage so you can talk to your disciple about their significance. The first book in this discipleship series, *Crowned: Created for Glory, Called by His Name*, is designed to help new believers and women lacking a Bible background become familiarized with the key doctrinal words concerning our identity in Christ. Refer to *Crowned* if you need to brush up on the meaning of words like salvation, sanctification, and justification.

As you train your disciple to study God's Word, encourage her in her discoveries. Help her add layers of depth to her task of observation by teaching her how to look up key words by using various Bible study tools like a Bible dictionary, concordance, and, as she gains confidence, even a lexicon. A user-friendly lexicon is located at the blueletterbible.org. On this site, you can look up a passage, click on specific words in the text, and discover how they are used in a sentence. Each of these resources communicates different information about how a word is used and its meaning.

In looking at Psalm 19, all these observations tools were helpful to me - the "W" questions, the key or repeated words, and the tenses of verbs. One of the "W" questions - "what" - led me to look at what God's Word is and what it does in our lives. Psalm 19 outlined several positive characteristics or descriptions of

God's Word that served as key words I needed to look up later (perfect, Law, sure, right, true, etc.,) in my Bible dictionary, concordance, or other Bible study tool. I also noticed several positive effects from God's Word that I needed to define (reviving, rejoicing, cleansing, etc.,).

POSITIVE CHARACTERISTICS	POSITIVE EFFECTS
Perfect	Revives the soul
Sure	Makes wise the simple
Right	Gladdens the heart
Pure	Enlightens the eyes
True	Keeps us from sin
Righteous	Cleanses us from sin Rewards us in him

But my studies into Psalm 19 didn't stop with key words or the answers to the "W" questions although, if they had stopped here, I would have had a great handle on the passage. But, as growing students of the Word, we have another important tool in our arsenal.

Grammar & Structure

When you've mastered the five "W" questions and

discerned the key words in a passage, try adding an additional layer to your Bible study skills by looking at the grammar and sentence structure used in a text. Grammar and structure are important because they reveal how key words are used in a passage. While some grammatical clues are hidden in the Bible's original languages, we can still gather a wealth of clues from our modern English translations.

When you're searching for grammatical and structural clues, you're charting out the structure of a sentence, paragraph, or passage. The most precise way to hunt for these types of clues is to actually diagram a sentence. Many of you may remember diagramming in English class; some of you may have purposefully blocked that part of your education from your memory.[35]

If you're anything like me, diagramming doesn't make your heart sing, but this truly is a helpful way to investigate a passage. I might not diagram a passage during my morning devotions, but if I'm preparing to teach a passage, I will do a diagram "short hand" that looks more like block diagramming.

And while I'm sure my high school English teacher would be horrified, I'll show you my process. On a separate piece of paper, I copy the passage from a website such as Biblegateway.com. Then I break each sentence into its natural phrases and clauses as I paste it – sticking to main clauses and subordinate clauses. I will indent each successive phrase and paste it on a different line to see the progression of a sentence.

Here's what my notes for studying Psalm 19:7 looked like when I began:

The law of the Lord

    is perfect,

        reviving the soul;

the testimony of the Lord

    is sure,

        making wise the simple;

There are many reasons to take a closer look at grammar and sentence structure by breaking apart a sentence into its basic phrases. In these structures, I can more easily identify all the grammatical tidbits that can get lost in a basic reading of the text. I look for the following in my phrases: subject (who is doing the acting), the direct object (who is being acted upon), verbs (action words), modifiers (adjectives/adverbs), prepositional phrases, and even connectors (and, but, therefore).

Looking at sentence structure isn't just about labeling words as nouns, verb, or ferreting out the direct object in a sentence. Breaking apart phrases and clauses is helpful for understanding how a key term is used in the surrounding sentence and discerning parallel themes in a story. You can see how the author is building his case or bolstering his claim right before your eyes. Is his claim positioned in a promise, command, or a conditional statement? Most importantly, however, the way a passage is structured can impact the meaning of a text, something we'll pick up in chapter 3 when we talk about context! So, don't give up on structure and grammar. Very often these types of searches will yield some important clues the author is embedding in his story for you to find!

GETTING A SYSTEM

To help you organize the facts you've gathered and to ensure you don't miss any clues along the way, get a system that works for you! There are dozens of systems you can use, and none is better than the other. It all depends on your personality and learning type. But above all, choose a system that makes sense to you and you can use consistently. If your system stresses you out, ditch it and find one that causes you to delight in God's Word! Here are a few systems that are commonly used to observe a text.

Print it

Print out a Bible passage on a separate piece of paper by copying and pasting from a website like Biblegateway.com. Because you can double space your lines, you'll have plenty of room to make notes and mark up your text. This method is a must if you're studying grammar and sentence structure!

When I'm studying a passage in-depth, adding a bunch of different observation layers, I like the print-out-method. I did this to research and write about Psalm 19 for this study, and it was helpful to have the extra space to make notes, draw pictures, and write in definitions of key words.

If you don't like the idea of keeping up with all those pieces of paper, you can also copy and paste your text in an app like Evernote. Sometimes in my quiet times, I will make notes using this app, which I love because it has a searchable feature and all my notes are saved. I can email them to myself later if I'm writing on a certain subject.

Code it

Some prefer to code their notes with colors or with symbols. This system works well if you are a visual person and enjoy working directly on the pages of your Bible. Bible study giants like Kay Arthur advocate using this system, encouraging students to color and code words with symbols using pencils or special Bible highlighters that don't bleed through the next page. Some of the symbols Kay invites you to use are triangles over the word "God" or megaphones each time you spot the word "gospel."

The color and code method is helpful for keeping your attention while reading and for discerning key themes over a large amount of Scripture as a certain color repeatedly pops up. If you like writing in your Bible, consider purchasing a Bible with extra wide margins for this method.

The coding method is wildly popular with many serious Bible study students. However, if you are a person who is easily stressed, I'd start out with a simpler system rather than having to learn a long list of symbols or try to keep your colors straight. For instance, start out by selecting a specific color for each of the five "W" questions.

In my personal devotions, I don't typically write a lot in my everyday Bible. I want my devotions to be fresh each time I read a passage, and personally, I find that colors and symbols marked in my Bible can distract me from seeing new things the Spirit might be revealing to me. Plus, because I retain what I learn by taking notes, I will eventually run out of room in the margins of my Bible to make notes.

Free-hand it

When I first began studying the Scriptures, I used the print-it-out method. It allowed me to be both thorough and systematic in making observations. But I soon discovered that the depth of my observations varied too greatly between when I was studying to teach a passage and when I was studying in my morning devotions. My teaching preparation time was rich with spiritual meat, but my devotions left me feeling unfilled. This bothered me because I wanted my morning devotions to be full of spiritual fruit. However, with young kids at home and the rush of school and lunchbox duty in the morning, I found I didn't have adequate time to copy, paste, and print out a passage for diagramming sentences each morning.

As a result, I came up with a worksheet template for my morning devotions. You can download a free PDF of the template on the *Sweeter than Honey* page of my site. The template can be used for any passage in the Bible, and provides space for working through each of the three components of the observation-interpretation-application method. Each section prompts me to look for all the important clues we've discussed in this chapter, plus the additional steps we'll uncover later. I usually print off about 25 pages at a

time and put them in a three-ring binder so they are
ready to be used when I wake up. There's no fumbling
with the printer while I'm still bleary-eyed, nor do I
have to look up reminders for what I'm supposed to
be observing in a text.

The template has done more for me than simply
making my morning devotions easier and richer; it has
also helped give me a broader understanding of the
story of the Bible. Let me explain. When I began to
study the Bible for myself, I quickly became an advocate for reading a book of the Bible in its entire context (which we'll talk more about in the next chapter).
For my morning devotions, I will commit to work
through a specific book of the Bible from beginning to
end, working on a little bit each day. I have no timeline
to complete the book, but move on only when I'm
ready.

The worksheets, all collected in one binder, allow
me to keep track of common themes and messages
that keep popping up in my studies, and I gain greater
insight into how the author fits specifics themes together through the course of his book or letter. So, by
the end of my readings, I've gathered a sizeable collection of observations about that particular book of the
Bible. Much like reviewing the praises and answered
prayers you've recorded in a prayer journal, my Bible
study binder helps me understand the greater story
behind God's Word. So, don't throw away any of your
observations, even if you think they aren't very insight-
ful. Keep them tucked away for future reference, or
for the next time you study the same book of the Bible. It is a blessing to be reminded of what truths the
Spirit showed you the first time you read the book, and

to track new things he shows you each time you work through it.

Plus, the more you practice spending time in God's Word, the more you can "free hand" your investigation. Because I've become so accustomed to using my Bible study template, I no longer need to be prompted to search for the five "W" questions or what terms and grammar tidbits to jot down. However, I still write out each of these observations because the process of doing so forces me to think clearly about the text.

Where to start

For new Bible students, I suggest you start out by working with shorter passages or even smaller sections in a chapter. What book should you start with? The Gospels (Matthew, Mark, Luke, and John) are always good books to begin your Bible study journey because they contain easy-to-follow stories. After you've selected and prayerfully read your passage through once, practice your observation skills using the five "W" questions. Then, identify key words and thoughts that are repeated in the passage. As you grow in your confidence and skill in uncovering these details, try moving onto grammar and sentence structure by breaking apart the sentence into phrases.

Once these types of investigations are mastered, more experienced Bible students can begin to look for more clues on their own. My Bible study template has a limited amount of space, but by putting these worksheets in a three-ring binder, you can use the back side of the previous piece of paper to make notes as well. I use this blank piece of paper to make lists I see forming in the text or to sketch out timelines for a story. I like to make charts or tables listing all the commands given in a text, the reason a command is given, and the result of keeping or disobeying these commands. I also use this blank space to write out questions brought up by the text that I want to circle back to later.

Here are some examples. In John 15:9-17, I made a chart with three columns. In each column, I wrote down truths about the Father, Son, and myself. I looked at actions, responses, and results. Last, I drew some key comparisons using Christ as my example.

JOHN 15:9-17

FATHER	SON	ME
Loves the Son	**To the Father:**	Abide in love
Gives commands	Abides in the Father's love	Obey him
Reveals himself	Keeps his Father's commands	Possess joy
	To us:	Love others
	Loves us	Bear fruit in him
	Serves us	Ask boldly
	Reveals the Father to us	
	Chooses us	
KEY: Jesus is the pattern for abundant life. Abundant life is living out the pattern of Jesus' life.		

In 1 Peter 2:1-3, I charted the progression of our personal transformation in Christ. I made a list of "old desires" and then a list of "new desires" we experience because of Christ. Next, I listed the result of those new desires in our lives and the reason for that transformation in our lives. From all that, I derived a key thought (which we'll talk more about in the next chapter).

1 PETER 2:1-3

OLD DESIRES	NEW DESIRES	RESULT	REASON
malice deceit hypocrisy envy slander	pure milk of the Word	so you may grow in salvation	"if" you have tasted the Lord's goodness

KEY: *Tasting God's grace changes us. It cultivates in us an appetite for God's Word and his ways.*

If you aren't sure what sort of chart to make or what you should include in your list, then try asking questions about the text. For instance, in my studies of the book of Hebrews, I found the amount of information too overwhelming to put into charts or lists. I was afraid I was missing something. So, I began my observations but asking questions.

For instance, in Hebrews 2:1-4 I asked myself, "why is God's Word trustworthy?" To answer that question, I made a list of how God's Word was described and what it accomplished. In Hebrews 5:5-11, I asked the question, "who is Melchizedek?" In answering that question, I made a list of how he was described and what he did. In Hebrews 6, the author speaks about the promises of God in Christ. I wondered what those promises were and then made a list of the specific promises that appeared in the text.

In Old Testament books comprised mostly of stories, try making lists about characters detailing who they are, what they said, and how they acted. Look at key events and the order in which they happened.

Sketch timelines to help you see the order of events clearly.

In stories, be sure to compare characters in a passage, especially if God is included. For instance, in my studies of Exodus, I found that most of my charts included some variation of the following headings: what God did, what God said, and Israel's response.

EXODUS 14:1-13

WHAT GOD SAID	WHAT GOD DID & WHY	ISRAEL'S RESPONSE
Camp near the sea Prepared them for adversity	Hardens Pharaoh's heart (so he gains HONOR & Egypt KNOWS he is Yahweh)	Went out boldly Became afraid when they saw Egypt Cried out to God Declared allegiance to Egypt instead of God
KEY: We will serve whom or what we fear. The true nature of our hearts (what we truly fear) is revealed when we are led to dead-ends of life.		

Lately, I've been doodling or lettering a phrase from the text that the Spirit causes to jump off the page. Creating picture-perfect artwork isn't my primary goal, but for some, visual aids help them retain what they've studied or help them enter into worship.

And while some people appreciate more specific guides that list the things they need to search for, I've discovered this "free hand" type system has yielded rich fruit for me that I can chew on throughout the day. So, after you've mastered the basics listed in this chapter, you might give this "free hand" approach to observation a try. But whether you use my system or another one, I can't underscore the value of putting your own system in place. Creating your own Bible study system will help train your eye to "see" the facts that are there, as well as help you establish a natural rhythm for studying the Scriptures.

The key to getting started is to start simple, adding layers of observation as you grow in your confidence and skill level in reading God's Word. Your efforts to pursue God's truth will not be in vain. God always shows up where we seek to know him through his Word. He promises us in the book of Isaiah that his Word never returns void. Isaiah 55:11 says, *"For as the rain and the snow come down from heaven and do not return there but water the earth, making it bring forth and sprout, giving seed to the sower and bread to the eater, so shall my word be that goes out from my mouth; it shall not return to me empty, but it shall accomplish that which I purpose, and shall succeed in the thing for which I sent it."*

Ready to dig in? Read Mark 8:22-25 – a passage we'll be studying in the next few chapters – and record your observations. Do not be tempted to speed through this part of the Bible study process. Remember, we said that observation is the most important part of digging into God's Word because how well you observe a passage determines how well you will interpret it and apply it to your life. Observation is the foundation of our Bible study investigation.

Pencil:
1. Gold yellow
2. 6 sides
3. Smooth
4. Lead inside
5. Has eraser on top
6. Metal band between eraser & pencil
7. Made of wood & rough w/ lines
8. Words imprinted below band = just basics
9. Words are printed, upper case & black
10. Eraser is orange
11. Eraser is round

CHAPTER 3 DISCUSSION QUESTIONS

1. What is Whiplash Wilma's approach to Bible study and do you resemble her? Why or why not? yes q no

2. Penciled in: in five minutes, make as many observations as you can about a No. 2 pencil. If applicable, share your observations with your group.

3. Read Mark 8:22-25, writing down your observations. First-time students: begin by asking the five "W" questions. If it seems easier, break the passage into phrases and look for grammar and sentence structure clues. For extra brave souls, free-hand your observations about the passage on a separate piece of paper. Be sure to share your findings if you are working in a group.

OBSERVATION? WHAT DO I SEE?

W hn Jesus & disciples come to Bethead a
people brought

Who: a blind man to him

What: begged Jesus to heal him
spat on eyes

When: during the day

Where: outside the village

Why: People were begging
Jesus healed blind man
& told him to go to his
home & not to the village
because people wouldn't
believe Jesus healed him

Genuine Faith Results

Praise glory & honor when JC
is revealed

FEAST WITH ME

On a separate piece of paper, spend some time with your disciple "free-handing" your observations of the following passages.[36]

Read John 19. Draw a chart with two columns. In one column, list the things done *to* Jesus. On the other side, list what Jesus did *for others*.

Read 1 Peter 1:1-12. Make a list of the results of genuine faith.

Read Hebrews 7:20-28. Draw a chart with two columns. In the first column, make notes about the old covenant. On the other side, make notes about the new covenant. Compare the two columns, noting which covenant is better and why.

DONE TO J

1. Flogged
2. Put crown of thorns on his head
3. Put purple robe on J
4. Struck in face
5. Chief priest + officials shouted "Crucify"
6. Gave Jesus vinegar to drink

JESUS DID

1. Claims to be Son of God
2. Didn't answer Pilate
3. Carried his cross
4. Told his mom + John that John was to care for her

The role of prayer in Bible study

Psalm 119 is the longest chapter in the entire Bible and extols the majesty of God's Word. Listen to how the Psalmist connects prayer and Bible study in Ps. 119:27, *"Make me understand the way of your precepts, and I will meditate on your wondrous works."*

The Psalmist is a prayer-saturated Bible reader. He begins his study of God's Word with prayer and continues that prayer throughout the day as he goes about his work. He is mulling over what he has read, thinking on it, marveling at it, celebrating it. I can imagine he's thinking on God's Word as he's harvesting wheat in the fields or walking dusty roads to the temple.

Ps. 119:34-36 continues, *"Give me understanding, that I may keep your law and observe it with my whole heart. Lead me in the path of your commandments, for I delight in it. Incline my heart to your testimonies, and not to selfish gain!"*

The Psalmist prays for God to give him understanding so that he might keep God's Word, observe it, and delight in it, all for God's glory. His requests for understanding center on the orientation of his heart. He doesn't just pray for knowledge; he prays for transformation. He is praying for God to change the craving cycle of God's Word in his life (attitude, appetite, and aim).

We must read the Scriptures prayerfully knowing that the Bible is God's Word to us. In prayer, we continue that conversation; prayer in Bible study is our heart response to God. So, when we read the Scriptures, we shouldn't just pray to understand them, we should pray as the Psalmist prays, that God's Word would penetrate and rightly align our hearts to his heart.

CHAPTER 4

INTERPRETATION: WHAT DOES IT SAY?

 Recently, an online picture of a dress went viral when a woman posted it with this question: "What color is this dress?" Some said the dress appeared black and blue. Others claimed the dress was white and gold. Obviously, both groups couldn't be right at the same time, and a big kerfuffle ensued over who had correctly interpreted the picture. The debate over the color of the dress garnered so much attention, that the dress manufacturer capitalized on its unexpected publicity and began to make the dress in both colors.

The second part of this Bible study strategy is interpretation. After you gather up all the facts you've observed, interpretation looks at meaning. Interpretation asks, "What does this passage say?" Or "What does it mean?" Just like observation, we can easily neglect this part of Bible study because we tend to think interpretation can be a little subjective.

a based on our personal feelings or views

Just like deciding if the color of the dress is black and blue or gold and white, we can too easily approach God's Word in the same way, arguing over the true meaning behind a verse. When we disagree about what a verse means, we often hear or say phrases like, "Well, that's just *your* interpretation" as if we can all be right at the same time.

This is a gross misunderstanding of what interpretation means. Because here's the thing, interpretation is not as subjective as you think. This is a biggie because people often use this excuse as a reason to avoid studying the Bible. They say: "Well, since no one can agree on how to rightly interpret the Scriptures, then we can't really know what it says." Do you know what I say to that? Hogwash. Rubbish. Hogswalup. Baloney!

Many of you have probably heard the illustration of six blind men who were asked to put their hands on an elephant and try to guess what it was. They observed the object using their remaining senses - touching, feeling, smelling, (we hope not tasting) - and then offered some interpretations. The first man felt the belly and said it was a wall. The second man felt the elephant's ear and determined it was a leathery fan. The third man felt the tail and surmised it was a rope, and so forth. Each man came up with a different interpretation based on his limited perception. The supposed point of that story is there are numerous ways to interpret God's Word, and because we all have different viewpoints – and here's the kicker – none of our interpretations are entirely accurate. Our culture would have you believe, based on that one illustration, that God's Word can be made to mean whatever someone wants it to mean.

But here's the problem with that story. Don't fall for it. In his book *Taking God At His Word,* author Kevin DeYoung proposes this "earth-shattering proposition."[37] What if the elephant can talk? What if the elephant can talk to the men who are feeling around, who are finite in their understanding, and can corroborate and correct their findings? What if he just whispers, "Hey, man, I'm an elephant," or more likely, he trumpets so they all know, "Oh, that's an elephant, not a rope, or a wall, or a fan like we thought!"

There will always be barriers to interpretation – language, culture, age, even our own wisdom levels. Our finite brains just can't grasp the fullness of God's glory. But we can't forget that the God of the Bible speaks! He has revealed himself in a specific message and because of that, his Word is a worthy revelation of himself. When we try to interpret God's Word, we might come up with different interpretations, but we aren't left in the dark to discern which interpretation is accurate because God speaks. And when he speaks, he is clear. So, overall ladies, the task of interpretation is not as subjective as you think.

Howard Hendricks puts it this way: "'Meaning' is not our subjective thoughts read into the text but God's objective truth read out of the text."[38]

impartial
unbiased

SAFEGUARDING YOUR INTERPRETATION

So, how do you ensure your interpretation of a passage is accurate? How can we be sure we are reading the truth that is already there and not just inserting our own truth? I want to give you three safeguards for ensuring your interpretation is accurate.

"Bee" sure to let Scripture speak for itself

The first rule of interpretation is to let Scripture speak for itself. By this I mean we always let Scripture interpret Scripture. For instance, when we come to a passage that perplexes us or seems contradictory, then we go to another part of Scripture to help explain it. We do not need to shy away from difficult passages. The Word of God is robust; it is hearty enough to withstand our inquiry! However, we always interpret difficult passages in light of clear ones. This also means we don't build entire doctrines around one verse, but rather, in light of the larger pattern and counsel of Scripture.

"Bee" faithful to the author's intent

The second safeguard for interpretation is to be faithful to the author's intent in writing. Okay, if there is one thing I want you take away from this chapter, it's what I'm about to tell you in the next few pages. So, listen up, look alive, give me some eyeball-to-eyeball action here. *If you will stick to the author's intent in writing when you are interpreting a passage, it will safeguard you from getting stung!* Here's what I mean. The author had a purpose for writing, and that purpose is the key to interpreting his message. We call this *authorial intent*. And it makes all the difference in interpreting a passage correctly!

In college, I took some feminist literary classes. They were interesting, but the way they reviewed novels always bothered me. I didn't figure out why their method bugged me so much until I got to seminary, and I realized the fatal flaw in how they read and interpreted a book. For example, 9 times out of 10, here's how our book discussions would go:

Student: *"I really like how the author used the color red throughout the story. The house was red. The main character wore a lot of red."* (Observation)

Teacher: *"Yes, that's a good observation! What do you think the color red signifies in the story?"* (Interpretation)

Student: *"Well, it's common knowledge that the color red symbolizes a woman's menstrual cycle and the pain that comes with our monthly period. So, I think the author is making a statement about the oppression and pain women feel at the hands of men in our society when she uses the color red."*

Me (on the back row): "*Huh?*"

I always left those classrooms feeling like I had interpretative whiplash, like we had missed the main point of the story and somehow had damaged the book the author really intended to write. Maybe the author used the color red for that reason, but maybe she didn't. Maybe red truly was symbolic, but for a different reason. Maybe she just really liked the color red. And if the color red wasn't significant, what *was* the real message of the book?

Are you tracking me? However, it wasn't until I got to seminary that I was able to pinpoint the reason I felt uncomfortable with this line of interpretation. It put the reader into the position of determining the meaning of the text, rather than reading the meaning that was already there. The reader allowed her experience to frame the meaning rather than the author's intent in writing. While personal experience can be helpful in engaging a literary work or a story, it is not our sole or even primary way to engage the biblical text.

In the last chapter, we were introduced to Whiplash Wilma – a woman bulldozing her way to the application part of Bible study. In interpretation, we meet her sister, Whiplash Wanda, a woman who misreads the signs on the road so badly that she changes lanes and gets off track. When you see Wanda doing wheelies in the parking lot, get out of her way because she is about to crash! Whiplash Wanda is just as dangerous as her heavy-footed sister; both do irreparable damage to the text and lives along the way.

Ladies, when we are interpreting a passage, our primary endeavor is to look for the author's purpose in writing. This is not as subjective of a process as we may think because if we agree that God inspired men to write a specific message, then we should be able to extract that meaning from the text.

You don't have to pull this from thin air. The author will give us clues as to his purpose, clues we uncover in the observation part of our study. These clues can be the words he uses, how he uses them, and how often he uses them. Even the way he orders the events of his story provides clues as to what truth he might be emphasizing. So, the more work we do in observation, the more faithful we can be to the author's intended meaning.

Let's take Mark 8 as an example. We made some

observations about this passage in the previous chapter. There was a repeated theme of sight. The author described the healing of a blind man using key and repeated words such as blind, eyes, see, and sight. You might not think too much about those words at first, but then there's this funny little exchange that sticks out in verses 23-24. The first time Jesus touches the man, the man still can't see clearly. When he opens his eyes, everything is still fuzzy.

What is going on here? Because when Jesus does something it usually sticks, right? Jesus didn't stand at the grave hollering for Lazarus before he was finally sauntered out, resurrected to life. Unlike moms everywhere, Jesus didn't use his middle name: "Lazarus James, you get out here right now!" Lazarus came out of the tomb immediately, the first time (John 11). Jesus got it right the first time.

In the story of the bleeding woman, it only took the woman reaching out to touch the hem of Jesus' garment for power to go out from his body. She was healed instantly. She didn't have to rip off a piece of his robe and rub it three times each day to receive his power (Luke 8:43-48). So, if Jesus wanted to restore this man instantly, he could have. So, what is going on here? I think the author is trying to get our attention. He is trying to slow us down long enough for us to wonder if there is something else at stake in this passage besides physical sight.

That question is answered for us when we back up and look at the context of the passage. So, I'm leaving you on a bit of a cliffhanger for Mark 8. We will come back to it, don't worry, but all I want to say right here is "bee" faithful to the author's intent when interpreting a passage. Look for clues the author leaves behind as to his intent.

"Bee" aware of context

I've already hinted at the third and final safeguard in interpreting a passage which is to be aware of context. There are three types of context I want to alert you to: historical context, immediate context, and the big picture context. All three types are crucial in interpreting a passage correctly. Let's look at each.

Historical Context

When we read a book or passage in the Bible, we must consider its historical context. We must acknowledge that the biblical authors wrote in a specific time in history. That means the background of a book or passage is important to consider when we begin to interpret a passage. You may have already uncovered some of this in observation, but when looking at the historical context, we must ask ourselves these questions:

(1) *Who was the author writing for or to?*

(2) *When were they writing?* Was it during a rebellion or a time of peace? What is the political context? Were they living under a king and was it a good king?

(3) *Where were they writing?* Was it while they were sitting on the heights of a throne or while rotting in the depths of a prison? Don't forget that the Bible was written by kings and paupers

      alike and people who held every job in be-
      tween.

(4) Why were they writing? Were they recording a sto-
      ry, investigating something, negating false
      teaching?

Any book lover will tell you backstory matters. Historical context will impact the way you read a passage.

In the first few chapters, we looked at Psalm 19.
Turn to that passage once again, and let's see what sort
of historical context we can dig up. At the very beginning of the chapter, you'll see a title. What does it say?
"To the choirmaster. A Psalm of David." So the title tells us
that this psalm was originally written for the Israelite
choirmaster. Presumably this psalm was originally written as a song to be sung by a chorus of voices. Does
that impact how you view this chapter? It probably
should! We should be rejoicing and singing for joy
about the God who reveals himself to us. We don't
just take away facts about God's Word (what it is and
what it does in our life), but rejoicing in its truth and
the hope it brings to our daily life.

Next, let's look at who wrote this song - David, a
King, whom Scripture describes elsewhere as a man
after God's own heart (Acts. 13:22). This is timely
news for us because David is also known for big fail-
ures. Despite being picked by God to be a forerunner
of Christ, David messed up in some very public and
painful ways. In some measure, we can all relate to
someone who has messed up their life beyond repair.
Further, if we were to continue to read the book of
Psalms, we'd discover that many of the Davidic psalms
correlate to a specific event in his life. When we read

contextually, we are looking for clues as to what was going on in the author's life at the time he was writing. Was he grieving the consequences of his own sin like David was when he wrote Psalm 51? Had he just been betrayed by a close confidant or family member like when he wrote Psalm 3?

All that background information (author, location, date, etc.) impacts the truth we glean from the Scriptures. Unless the author gives us a clue as to all this, we might have to go to a secondary source to get the entire historical context.

Bibles that are specifically labeled as study Bibles will include an introduction to each book that outlines background information. If you have one of these Bibles, you'll find the introduction at the beginning of each book. When you read a passage, very quickly turn to that page so you can get the contextual gist of what's going on. Additionally, a sound study Bible will provide additional information and explanatory notes in the margins or footnotes.

Immediate Context

To read contextually, we must also consider the immediate context of a passage. That means, don't just read one verse and expect to understand it. Reading contextually means we must read what immediately precedes or follows a passage. For instance, if you are trying to interpret a passage, be sure to read the whole paragraph around a verse, read the entire chapter, and then read the whole book. My two favorite parts of the Bible to practice reading contextually is in the Gospels and the Psalms – two parts of Scripture that we often do the most damage contextually. The Gospels give accounts of Jesus's earthly life and ministry. Too commonly, we read stories from the Gospels without any thought to how the author ordered them. Our studies in Mark will prove that the order of events matters! The same is true of the Psalms; we read one psalm here and there without thinking about where it was situated in the whole book.

Very quickly, I'll walk you through this type of contextual look at Psalm 19. If you were to look at the Psalms that precede and follow it (Ps. 18 and Ps. 20), you'll find that both speak of God in royal terms. Psalm 18 shares an Easter story, the story of a King and priest who tasted death on the people's behalf so they might taste his righteousness, after which he ushers in a new kingdom. In Psalm 20, we see a picture of an anointed King who is coming to save and who calls us personally.

Going further, Psalm 21 celebrates the victory won by the King of which his people enjoy. Then Psalm 22 sings a song of suffering in which the anointed One, the Messiah, endures great affliction. So by the time you reach Psalm 23, the Psalmist is speaking of the Good Shepherd and how God relates to his people. Finally, Psalm 24 speaks of the King's kingdom again.[39]

I tell you all this because this should impact the way we interpret Psalm 19. We cannot interpret Psalm 19, which is sandwiched between two royal psalms and clearly pointing to the coming Savior, without thinking of the coming King, the anointed One, who is the perfect revelation of God (Heb. 1:1-2:4). It's why I spent so much time talking about Christ, who is the Living

Word, in chapter 2. I did that because the final editors who ordered the Psalms in a meaningful way believed Psalm 19 to speak ultimately of Christ. That meaning was already there in Psalm 19. In this way, we aren't reading something into the text that isn't there. It is too easy to read Christ back into the Old Testament, but rather, reading contextually means we are reading what already *is* there in the correct way.

To interpret a passage correctly and in line with the author's intent, we must look at the immediate context of the passage. Context impacts our interpretation. It helps us see exactly what the author's purpose was in writing. Don't isolate a verse from its paragraph or a chapter from its entire book. Spend some time looking around, lest you become like Whiplash Wanda.

Remember our Mark 8 cliffhanger when we were discussing the author's intent in writing? Now that we've talked a little bit about interpreting a passage based on its immediate context, I want to circle back to Mark 8. Let's walk through Mark 8 together and see what insights we glean that will impact the meaning of that text for us. There is space in the discussion questions at the end of this chapter to record your notes.

In Mark 8:22-25, we have the story of a blind man who is healed. His sight is restored to him by Christ. Now, let's practice reading that passage contextually. Go back to the beginning of Mark 8, and look at the title of that first section in verses 1-10. What event does it record? The feeding of the 4,000. So, Jesus performed a miracle for all to see that he was the Messiah.

Now, move on to the next section in verses 11-12. The title is "The Pharisees seek a sign." Verse 11 says, *"Then the Pharisees came out and began to dispute with Him, seeking from Him a sign from heaven, testing Him."* Evidently, the Pharisees didn't have their glasses on because they missed the huge, blinking sign Jesus provided in the previous verses (i.e. multiplying enough fish and bread for 4-5,000 peeps). So, the Pharisees seem to have a bit of a sight problem.

Now, move on to the next section in verses 13-21. What's going on here? Jesus leaves with his disciples on a boat to go to the other side of the lake. When they arrive, the disciples look around and realize they forgot to bring their doggie bags from the feeding of the 4,000. They *"forgot to take bread,"* the sign Jesus provided to point to his deity (see verse 14). They are probably muttering about the silly bread, and Jesus rebukes them: "Hey, it's not about the bread, guys." In verse 18, Jesus says, *"Having eyes, do you not see?... How is it you do not understand?"* He's asking them, "You saw first-hand what I can do, so why don't you trust me to provide for you now?"

Are you noticing a theme take shape in Mark 8? Sight is not just physical sight. The author is weaving these individual stories together to make a larger point about our spiritual eyesight and how it impacts our belief and trust in Him.

Sketching out the order of events is helpful when considering context. Look carefully at each individual or group's response to Jesus.

MARK 8 IN CONTEXT

Vs.1-10	Vs. 11-12	Vs.13-21	Vs. 22-25
Who: Jesus	**Who**: Pharisees	**Who:** Disciples	**Who**: Blind man
What: Feeds 4,000 (a sign)	**What:** Need a sign to believe	**What:** Miss seeing the sign clearly	**What:** Eyesight healed by Christ
Why: The sign proves he is the Christ	**Why**: They are blind to belief	**Why**: They lack spiritual eyes & true understanding	**Why:** Sees physically, but not spiritually

Our contextual reading leads us to this main question: is seeing believing? In Mark 8:1-10, Jesus provides a sign that he is the Messiah. Mark 8:11-12 records the Pharisees' response; they are blind to belief and miss "seeing" or interpreting the signs correctly. In Mark 8:13-21, the disciples see the sign, but still lack true understanding. Then comes the story of the actual blind man whose sight is restored in Mark 8:22-25. His very own eyes become a sign, but he is still spiritually blind because Jesus tells him in vs. 26: *"Go and don't tell anyone."* He clearly didn't understand what had happened to him.

The immediate context of Mark 8:22-25, then, is about more than a miracle proving Jesus is Christ; this passage speaks of the true nature of belief. Understanding who Christ is doesn't require physical proof or signs. True belief is undertaken by the spiritual eyes of our heart, which rightly perceive Christ to be the Son of God and trust in him (Eph. 1:18).

So, context changes how you interpret a passage. Before we looked at the immediate context of Mark 8, we would have thought the point of that story was just about Christ providing a physical sign that he was the Christ. However, after reading contextually, we discover the point of Mark 8:22-25 is actually the opposite! Context tells us that even those who have signs don't understand or fully believe. True belief comes from an internal understanding. Seeing isn't always believing.

Isn't this fun? Context is going to open your world when you read the Bible. So, in interpretation, we must safeguard our interpretation by reading contextually. If we read a passage out of context, we will very likely veer off course in interpreting it.

Big Picture Context

Finally, we must not only read the Bible for historical or immediate context, but also for the big picture context of Scripture. This means zooming out and using your wide angle lens when you're looking at a passage. Howard Hendricks calls this "reading telescopically" – reading the parts in light of the whole.[40]

When I say big picture, this is what I mean. The Bible is one, unified story. Yes, we often read the books of the Bible separately. But each book plays an important part in God's story for the world. God's story is the story of redemption – how God is at work in the world to redeem and restore it through his Son, Jesus Christ. We call this story the grand biblical narrative, and you can trace it from beginning to end, from Genesis all the way to Revelation. So it doesn't matter if you're reading about day 5 of Creation, how God provided manna in the wilderness, or how Paul deals with false teaching in his New Testament letters to the church; the Spirit is always pushing the reader toward redemption.

And that narrative – God's story – has four major plot moves: creation, fall, redemption, and restoration.

The first plot move is *creation*. In this part of the plot, a good King created a good world. Mankind is his crown on creation, created and commissioned to reign on earth under the King.

The second plot move is the *fall* – the good world God created becomes corrupted by sin. Creation rebels against the throne of God, failing in their calling to serve as the King's rulers on earth. They become separated from their King.

The third plot move is *redemption*, the climax of God's story for the world. The good King is at work to redeem his creation by sending his Son, Jesus. Through King Jesus, mankind is saved from the corruption of sin.

The final plot move is restoration. The King not only rescues mankind from the consequences of their rebellion, he restores them to their rightful place on the throne with him.

If you were to sum up the big picture context of Scripture in one sentence it would be this: *a good King created a good world, and although it was corrupted by sin, he is at work to redeem it and restore it through his Son, Jesus Christ.*

All Scripture speaks to this story. It doesn't matter if you're reading in the first book of the Bible, close to the end, or somewhere in the middle. All Scripture refers to and plays a part in the unfolding of this grand story. In each passage, then, we should be able to pick out some of these major plot moves. While you might not find all four plot moves in every single verse in the

119

Bible, reading with contextual eyes will guide you in finding several of them.

Let's try to do that with Psalm 19, re-reading with contextual eyes, looking for hints about the big picture. When you read the Psalms with big picture eyes, you'll be amazed at what truths you can glean from them. The Psalm begins by speaking about *creation*. Verses 1-6 tell us that God created a good world, and it all points to him and his goodness. Creation declares his glory (vs. 1).

Then beginning in verse 7, we see a shift in the language. It says God gave us a Law, and his Law is perfect. In contrast, Psalm 19 reveals we are not perfect. Elsewhere, Scripture says God gave us his Law to reveal our sin and our need for help (Rom. 3:20; 7:7-13). Because of the *fall*, things in this world are not as they should be. The Psalmist notes that everybody "errs" in verse 12, and this problem of sinning is something mankind can't fix on our own. We can't, as he says in verse 12, cleanse ourselves.

As we've already seen, verses 12-14 are a pretty important part of this song. In them, the Psalmist reveals that God is the one who cleanses us through *redemption*. In verse 13, we are declared blameless and innocent of transgression, and in verse 14, we are redeemed by him.

But the Psalmist doesn't stop with redemption. At the end of verse 14, he refers to *restoration*. In our observation process, we discovered that through the progression of discipleship, God is at work in us to make us look like him (vs. 7-11). He cleanses us through his Word. This is total transformation (soul, mind, heart, body), and the result is that we desire him – we crave his Word even more. As we become more like him, God's Word becomes to us sweeter than honey, which is what God wanted at the beginning of creation for his people. The result is we are made acceptable to God, restored to our original purpose. Psalm 19, then, is a song of restoration!

Wow! Did you think you were reading the New Testament? You aren't reading something into the text that isn't there. You aren't reading Christ back into the Old Testament. You aren't reading anything *into* the text; when you read contextually, you're reading what the author intended to convey.

Big picture eyes are helpful tools for keeping our eyes on the road before us. They help us remember God's plan of redemption no matter where we are reading in the Bible. Using these eyes can take practice, especially if you're a new Bible student. So, don't grow weary in learning how to read contextually. If you want to develop this particular skill, spend one week simply reading a Psalm a day using only your big picture eyes. In a journal, write out the four plot moves and make notes of where you see them in the text. You'll be surprised at how easy it will become for you to put on these wide angle lenses!

For more practice reading with contextual eyes, skip to the discussion questions at the end of the chapter and put your new eyes to work!

SUMMARIZE THE MAIN IDEA

So, now let's get to some nuts and bolts. How do we go about interpreting a passage or verse? *The easiest way to interpret a passage is to summarize its main idea.* That's right, we are going back to second grade English class. We are keeping it simple by taking all the facts we observed and boiling them down to get the main idea of the text. I'll use the abbreviation one of my seminary professors used: the main idea of the text is the MIT.[41]

Here's the key: the main idea (MIT) asks this question: "What was the main point *then*?" Interpretation is concerned with the past.[42] Later, in application, we'll jump to the present and ask "What is the point *now*?" But in interpretation mode, we're really just asking about the author's perspective. Remember we want to be faithful to the author's intent. What was the author's main point in writing this passage?

In this phase, we aren't just listing our observations or restating them. Rather, we are relaying what those observations mean. Using the method of that very same seminary professor, we'll ask two key questions to get the MIT.[43] The two key questions are: (1) what is the author talking about? And (2) what is the author *saying* about what he is talking about?

FINDING THE MAIN IDEA OF THE TEXT (MIT)

STEP 1: What is the author talking about? (What is the passage mostly about?)

STEP 2: What is the author saying about what he is talking about? (Add supporting details.)

STEP 3: Combine steps 1 & 2 into a single sentence to find the MIT. (Smoosh them!)

If you want to keep this even simpler, you can just

follow the basic second grade writing prompt: what is this passage mostly about? Then fill in some supporting details. These two key steps will help you discern the MIT.

Once you've answered those two key questions, you then do something very scholarly and very technical. Are you ready? You smoosh those two thoughts together to arrive at the main idea, your hard-earned interpretation. Yes, you smoosh them. I'm sure my seminary professor would be very impressed.

Before we dive in, I want to give you a few friendly tips. When you get to this part of the Bible study process, don't try to do this in your head. I still write out my findings to these three steps to discern the MIT, even if I think I already know the main idea. These three prompts are printed on my Bible study template, so each time I study a passage, I follow these exact steps. Why? They help me get to the heart of the message, and they keep me on track. Without them, I'd be doing wheelies in the parking lot.

Another tip: I always do my studies in pencil. Why? Because I don't want to stress to get this part of the process perfect on the first go. In fact, I spend a lot of time erasing and re-writing what I believe to be the main point or filling in supporting details I think are important. And you can bet that I spend a lot of time writing and re-writing as I try to "smoosh" the two steps together. Sometimes what I have sounds too rough, and I will refine and edit two or three times.

So, get your pens, journal, and paper, and starting writing things down as you study! Together, let's find the MIT of Psalm 19 by asking these two key interpretative questions and then smooshing our answers into a final sentence. But first, let's review some of the observations we dug up in Psalm 19 in the previous chapters.

POSITIVE CHARACTERISTICS	POSITIVE EFFECTS
Perfect	Revives the soul
Sure	Makes wise the simple
Right	Gladdens the heart
Pure	Enlightens the eyes
True	Keeps us from sin
Righteous	Cleanses us from sin Rewards us in him

In our studies, we observed that the author outlined the positive characteristics of God's Word and the many positive effects his Word produces in our life.

With that in mind, let's boil down all those observations to find the MIT of Psalm 19 using our two key questions. First, *what is the author talking about?* Here's how I answered that question: Psalm 19 is mostly about the positive and lasting qualities and effects of God's Word on mankind.

Now, let's ask the second question: *what is the biblical author saying about what he is talking about?* What are some of those supporting details? He is saying mankind needs God's Word in order to truly enjoy a life of joy and righteousness.

Now, in step three, let's get a little more succinct and combine those two thoughts to get the main idea. The main idea of Psalm 19 is God's Word is the only trustworthy source for experiencing abundant life. If you wanted to tighten that up more, you could also say, there is no sweeter source for abundant life than the Word of God.

That is the interpretation I used for our study in this book: *there is no sweeter source for abundant life than the Word of God.* Remember, we talked at great length about the sweetness of his Word and how God's Word was sweet. Either of those thoughts could serve as the MIT for Psalm 19. But the tighter your MIT is, the closer you get to producing a better, clearer summary!

THE MAIN IDEA (MIT) OF PSALM 19

STEP 1: What is the author talking about? *(What is the passage mostly about?)*

Psalm 19 is mostly about the positive and lasting qualities and effects of God's Word on mankind.

STEP 2: What is the author saying about what he is talking about? *(supporting details)*

Mankind needs God's Word in order to truly enjoy a life of joy and righteousness.

STEP 3: Combine steps 1 & 2 into a single sentence to find the MIT. *(Smoosh them!)*

God's Word is the only trustworthy source for experiencing abundant life.

So, interpretation is basically determining the MIT

in light of the passage's context. After looking at overall context, we work through the three-step process for finding the MIT.

In the notes at the end of this chapter, try to discern the MIT for Mark 8:22-25. If you can discern the main idea on your own, great! But if you're like me and find a guide helpful, try using the three-step process to help you. Above all, avoid doing wheelies in the parking lot by keeping your eyes on the signs around you! Whiplash Wilma and her twin sister, Wanda, are always lurking around the corner!

CHAPTER 4 DISCUSSION QUESTIONS

1. Practice reading God's Word with contextual eyes. Look up the background of Mark to get a sense of the *historical context*.

2. Practice reading for *immediate context*. Read the events before and after Mark 8:22-25. How do the individual stories in the chapter relate?

   feeding of 5,000 & who do you say I am & tells of his future miracles (eye sill restored

3. Read Mark 8:22-25 again looking for the *big picture context*. Note any of the big picture plot moves you spot in the passage (Hint: creation, fall, redemption, restoration).

4. Which of the above exercises in contextual reading impacted your interpretation of Mark 8:22-25 the most? *immediate*

5. Find the main idea of the text (MIT) for Mark 8:22-25 using the three-step method. *Jesus can heal at any time & anywhere see page 129 - next page*

Step 1: *What is the author talking about?* (What is the passage mostly about?)

miracle of healing

Step 2: *What is the author saying about what he is talking about?* (supporting details)

Jesus is who He say He is

Step 3: *Combine steps 1 & 2 into a single sentence to find the MIT.* (Smoosh them!)

Jesus is the Messiah & He will provide for us & heal us.

Holman Illustrated Bible Handbook

"VINES complete expository dictionary"

"Key Word Study Bible"

Just for fun. Are you on Twitter? For social media newbies, Twitter is a communication tool where users can post short status updates of 140 characters or less (including spaces!) Challenge your small group to edit their final MIT of Mark 8:22-25 to less than 140 characters and tweet it with #sweeterthanhoney. Then, hand out rewards for successful tweets!

FEAST WITH ME

Disciplers, spend some time helping your disciple familiarize herself with various study tools. Show her how to find the introduction of a book in a study Bible and what kind of contextual information it provides. Since we've been studying Psalm 19, have your disciple find the introduction to the Psalms and pick out key information needed to help interpret the passage.

While you're at it, bring a commentary and a Bible dictionary to your small group session and pass them around. Show new Bible students how to look up a passage or key words in both tools.

The role of the Holy Spirit in Bible study

If the Bible is our textbook, then the Holy Spirit is our teacher. God's Spirit teaches us by illuminating God's Word. The Holy Spirit guides us into truth in two ways.

First, the Holy Spirit illuminates our minds to the truth. As we read the Scriptures, he enlightens our eyes to understand what we're reading. First Cor. 2:8-10 says, *"But, as it is written, 'What no eye has seen, nor ear heard, nor the heart of man imagined, what God has prepared for those who love him' — these things God has revealed to us through the Spirit. For the Spirit searches everything, even the depths of God."* The Spirit searches the depths of God for us! Much like a highlighter that illuminates words on a page, the Spirit helps us to see clearly the truth that he has already inspired in the Scriptures.

Second, the Spirit awakens our hearts to love the Word even more. We are not called to crave God's Word for knowledge sake, but for application. Ps. 119:34 says, *"Give me understanding, that I may keep your law and observe it with my whole heart."* The Psalmist prays for a type of understanding that will change his heart. God did not give us the Illuminator and Teacher of Truth so we might know more truth, but so that we might walk in his truth. The Spirit illuminates the Word to us so we can both know God and walk in the ways of God.

CHAPTER 5

APPLICATION: WHAT DO I DO?

 Some of my favorite websites are sites dedicated to fails. Cake decorating fails. Clothing fails (which always seem to include leggings). And, of course, Pinterest fails. Can we talk about the Pinterest fails, please? Because Pinterest is like the fairy godmother of craft-challenged, uncreative women everywhere. She's a charlatan in Martha Stewart clothing. But for many of us who are desperate to be the belle of the ball at holiday gatherings (or our kid's first-grade class party), her spells usually go awry. Those dinner rolls shaped like adorable little Easter bunnies? When you take them out of the oven, those little ears you clipped into the dough will turn out looking like little horns. Trust me. And serving "devil" rolls at Easter brunch just won't do.

Much like Cinderella sitting in the middle of the road on top of a squashed pumpkin, moms everywhere are left to wonder at what stage did things go wrong when we followed the directions exactly. The

#nailedit hashtag has become, for many of us, a giant ironic joke! Pinterest really should look into branding this tagline: *Results May Vary*. Because we can follow the directions meticulously, yet an craft can easily turn out nothing like its picture. As women, we're hit with this reality every day.

The application of makeup? Yeah, results definitely vary. I tried a "smoky eye" once. I followed that tutorial step-by-step, but I looked like I had come out of a bar fight after getting doused with water and sleeping flat on my face for about 24 hours. I was going for Angelina Jolie, but what I got was night of the living dead instead. Results may vary? Yes, indeedy.

Doing laundry? I don't care what claims that Oxi-Clean™ infomercial makes, my whites turned the brightest shade of Pepto-Bismol® pink you've ever seen after "someone" added a red sock to the washer. That day, my results varied.

The reason results vary, even when we scrupulously follow the instructions, is because we all live in our own contexts. With respect to beauty products, I don't look like Angelina Jolie. I don't have makeup artists or stylists at my beck and call. And laundry? Well, that infomercial guy probably doesn't have a set of Weasley twins running interference for his household chores.

So, even if we truly might be following all the instructions, doing everything we're supposed to be doing, we all have our own unique life contexts. Each of us has her own calling and circumstances, people and problems in life. That's why, when we get to the process of application in Bible study, and we ask the question, "What do I do?" we will see the results will vary. Remember, while there is one interpretation of a passage, there can be many applications.

THE DIFFERENCE IS IN THE RESULTS

So, what difference does application make? Do we really need it? Yes! We do need application because *the difference is in the results.* Not only do we have to take into account our personal life context, but we also have to keep in mind that God is at work in our lives in different ways and at different times to grow us into the likeness of his Son.

Application, then, isn't just about doing the right thing or adding items to our to-do list. Here's the key: how well we apply biblical truth is tied directly to our spiritual health. In fact, spiritually healthy people will display three key markers in their lives.

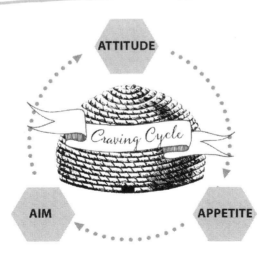

Spiritually healthy people eat well

In chapter 2, we talked about cultivating a craving for the sweetness of God's Word. We discovered that when we spend consistent time reading and studying God's Word, we remained fueled up for life and all its challenges.

And the more we desired to know God's Word, the more we wanted to feast on it. Like soda or potato chips, we get one taste and we're hooked. We crave it, so our attitudes and appetites grow proportionately. When we feast on God's Word, we are fueled up and ready to go, and the more we eat it, the more we'll crave it.

Spiritually healthy people exercise

But, in order to increase in our cravings, we can't stop there. Bible study is not simply about feasting on God's Word. This is the general principle at work in our faith: if we eat too much, we gain weight, right? In the same way that our bodies need physical exercise to be healthy, our spiritual bodies need exercise, too. Application is part of our spiritual exercise.

But if all we do is exercise (run here, do this, do that, cross off items from our to-do list), then we will get tired. Our fuel will eventually burn out, and we will be left feeling empty and exhausted. It is in those moments of ministry that we must take time to refuel. It is the natural cycle that demonstrates our level of spiritual health. If we don't exercise, the aim of God's Word is thwarted. We can become lazy, ineffective, and overweight. If we don't refuel on God's Word on a consistent basis, we will quickly tire and burn out. If we remove any part of this spiritual health cycle, we render ourselves ineffective.

This is where I want you to pay close attention. Because for those of us who have been around this track a few times, we can easily think we don't have to jump over all these hurdles. For instance, we can read a passage on honesty and when we get to the application part, all we do is pat ourselves on the back. If a passage calls us to exercise our faith by having an honest heart, we can think things like, "Awesome. I'm already doing that. I don't really lie to people." So, we don't really give our spiritual muscles a true work out. We don't spend the necessary time in our own personal context to examine our heart to discern where we might be lacking complete integrity.

As a result, we get stuck in this rut of non-change. Pretty soon we'll become so comfortable that we stop exercising altogether. So be sure to get a physical and consider where you tend to get stuck in the cycle of spiritual health.

Spiritually healthy people experience change

Spiritually healthy people eat well, exercise, and last, they see evidence of change. This process of diet and exercise is not entirely up to us. This is the key: *spiritually healthy people experience spiritual change, true and lasting change from the inside out.* The more we make the choice to apply God's Word (listen, love, obey), the more God shapes and directs our hearts to want to listen, love, obey. So, as we make our rotations around this cycle, God changes us. It is not that we are doing it, but God, by the power of his Spirit, is changing us to make us look more like him. He increases our cravings for spiritual truth. How well we apply biblical truth, then, is tied directly to our spiritual health.

RESULTS MAY VARY

In the last chapter, we noted that interpretation is concerned with the past. "What was the author saying, *then*?" But in application, we are going to bring the main idea of a text (MIT) into the present. In application, we lift a passage out of its historical context, and we position it in a modern context.

Regardless of context, the Bible is applicable and relevant today. Let's think about some of the big hot button life issues present in our culture today? I can hear these key words in a single news cycle: abortion, common core/education, daycare options, government healthcare, immigration, gender identity, and terrorism. However, if you were to open your Bible right now, you probably wouldn't find a passage that specifically addresses each of those topics using those labels.

Applications are based on principle

Some of the issues that we face in our culture today are not specifically addressed in the Bible. But here's why the Bible is still relevant today, and here's how we can apply the Bible in a modern context and still remain true to the author's purpose in writing: the Bible is based on principles, principles that touch on universal life issues felt by every person, around the globe. It doesn't matter if they lived 2,000 years ago or in the 21st century.

The Bible is relevant today because it offers *general principles* based on *universal, timeless truths*. The work of application in Bible study is to identify general principles and then draw out specific responses to those truths. Application asks the question, "What is God calling me to do in response?" It is this question that the Spirit uses to change us – from the inside out.

Commonly, however, we make one of two errors when we apply a text. First, we make our applications so vague that they aren't really applications. They are just mere principles (i.e.: "trust in the Lord," "believe," or "don't worry").

The second error we can make in applying a text takes us to the other end of the spectrum. We bypass the basic principle the passage addresses and go straight to the specifics. For example, we add unbending rules to everyday activities like we must pray three times a day for an hour each or we're "doing it wrong." Or, in Bible study, we must read 30 minutes or more in order to really be doing it right. This error treats a specific application like it's a universal truth for everyone.

Being too vague and too specific are both mistakes because either extreme can lead us to lazy religion or legalistic religion. When we're lazy, we don't push for real internal change demonstrated by the spiritual fruit of God's Word in our lives. When we're enslaved to legalism, we try to manufacture our own spiritual fruit.

So, when you begin the application process, the first step is to extract the overarching principle from the text. Begin by listing out some life issues you see in the passage and what the text says about them.

Commonly, these life issues might fall in line with the main idea of the text (MIT), particularly if you're looking at a verse or just a few verses like we've been practicing in Mark 8:22-25. For instance, in identifying the main principle behind Psalm 19, it followed closely with my MIT: God's Word is the only trustworthy source for a life of joy. But sometimes the principle is a bit more 'big picture,' especially if you're looking at an entire chapter (like Mark 8). This is where your observation and interpretation skills inform your application. Look carefully for key principles concerning God such as his character and activity.

Applications bring interpretations into the present

Now, once you have determined the general principle or life issue in a passage, you are ready to delve into specifics: "What do I do?" The key thought here is this: "How do I bring this principle into the *present*," into my personal context?

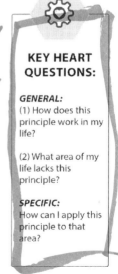

KEY HEART QUESTIONS:

GENERAL:
(1) How does this principle work in my life?

(2) What area of my life lacks this principle?

SPECIFIC:
How can I apply this principle to that area?

Results really do vary, and in a good way, because the Bible is a deeply personal, dynamic book. So, where there are more clear cut rules in observation and interpretation (looking for the context and the author's purpose/intent), in application we must learn to listen to the Spirit. And the best way to do that, to discern the specifics of how a passage applies to you, is to bombard the text with "how" questions. I suggest starting out with this key question: *How does this principle work in my life?* And then more specifically ask this follow-up question: *Is there an area of my life that lacks this principle?*

These are the questions I worked through in studying Psalm 19. First, I identified the main principle behind the passage: God's Word is the only trustworthy source for a life of joy.

Next, I peppered the text with general "how" questions. *How does this principle work in our lives?* We are meant to long for the Word of God over any other fleeting or temporal desire. *What area of my life lacks this principle?* The struggle to crave God's Word over other desires is a universal and timeless struggle even as the specific desires will vary. We outlined a few of the most common desires in chapters one and two – safety, beauty, power, wealth, affirmation, etc.

The final step in applying Psalm 19 required that I move to more specific applications, asking *how women might apply it to those lacking areas in their lives.* As the Spirit convicts us of what competing desire we are elevating above him in our hearts, a woman who craves the Word will need to confess and submit those offending desires over to God.

APPLYING PSALM 19
"What do I do?"

PRINCIPLE: God's Word is the only trustworthy source for a life of joy.

HEART QUESTIONS *(General)*:
(1) How does this principle work in my life?
I should long for the Word of God over other desires, viewing it as sweeter than honey.

(2) What area of my life lacks this principle?
I must identify competing desires feeding my soul, such as safety, pleasure, beauty, power, wealth, affirmation, and more.

HEART QUESTIONS *(Specific)*:
(3) How can I apply this principle to that area?
I must confess to God offending desires, consistently feed on God's Word, and submit to both its authority and correction in the Spirit.

Our application of Psalm might have ended there, but luckily, Psalm 19 offers its own applications for submitting for idolatrous desires to the cross. I outlined them in chapter 2 as the two key markers of a woman of the Word. First, a woman of the Word submits to the authority of the Word, trusting that it offers her the best way to live (Ps. 19:8-10). Second, a woman of the Word submits to the correction of the Word, by keeping her from sin and allowing it to cleanse of her sin in consistent study (Ps. 19:11-14).

Let's look at another quick example. Proverbs 22:6 is a well-known verse quoted by Christian parents around the globe. It says, *"Train up a child in the way he should go: and when he is old, he will not depart from it."*

When applied poorly, this passage can be wielded as both a terrible weapon and a warm coat to cover up guilt and shame. Scores of parents have faithfully and carefully trained their child in the ways of the Bible and, in the end, their child departed from it! So, what gives?

If there was ever a warning label that should be attached to a passage, it's this: results may vary! Proverbs 22:6 is commonly and mistakenly treated as a promise. If I do X, then Y is the guaranteed result. In this way, we try to manufacture our own fruit.

However, Proverbs 22:6 is a fabulous example of a basic principle for the life issue of parenting. It is a general guiding statement for life. Generally speaking, it is universally true, but it also means that results will vary, regardless of how diligent parents may be in raising children in the ways of God.

So what is the guiding principle behind this verse? Some of the life issues in Proverbs 22:6 might include the hard work of parenting, faithful Christianity, God's sovereignty over parenting, etc. So, generally speaking, parents who are faithful to raise their children in light of God's Word will see their children go on to be faithful to God's Word. Faithful parenting generally leads to biblically faithful children.

Notice I said, "generally speaking." We run into trouble, however, when we race straight away to the specifics: "I've got to read the Bible to my child every day, do family devotions, etc., in order for them to turn out right." The fruit yielded from such a path is not likely to last because it is self-manufactured. Self-manufactured fruit quickly leads us to the rocky road of legalism, a road which finds discouragement, disappointment, and disillusionment as its destination.

The principle we said emphasized the importance of faithful, biblical parenting. So, now let's ask our first general heart question: how does this work in my life? I'll bear my soul, here, and demonstrate how I would apply Proverbs 22:6 in my own personal context. (As you know, I have 8-year-old identical twin boys, so this question is not new to me). I'll begin by asking myself the "how" questions. *How does this principle of biblically faithful parenting work in my life?* First, in order for me to be a parent who faithfully teaches a child about the Bible and the God it is about, I need to know the Bible and the God it is about.

Specifically, how do I be a mom who knows the Bible and knows God? Here is my answer: in order for me to be a parent who is faithful to teach her child about the Bible and the God it's about, I need to spend time reading, studying, and applying God's Word. Notice that so far, my focus is not on my children, but on myself. *I* need to be faithful. So, from the principle of Proverbs 22:6, I've surmised that before I can expect my children to be faithful to God's Word, I need to be immersed in God's Word.

But let's get a little more specific than that. Now, I'll ask myself my final follow-up question: *Is there any area in my life that lacks this principle?* Again, this is where I really need to follow the Spirit's leading, asking for help in discerning areas in need of change and help in responding to his prompting.

144

APPLYING PROVERBS 22:6
"What do I do?"

PRINCIPLE: Biblically faithful parents generally produce biblically faithful children.

HEART QUESTIONS *(General)*:
(1) How does this principle work in my life?
To be a biblically faithful parent, I must be immersed in God's Word - studying it and applying it to my life.

(2) What area of my life lacks this principle?
To be a biblically faithful parent, I need to cooperate with the Spirit as his Word transforms my heart and sinful emotions.

HEART QUESTIONS *(Specific)*:
(3) How can I apply this principle to that area?
I must honestly identify sinful emotions and why I am feeling them. With the Spirit's help, I must surrender and the sinful desires of my heart to him.

So, at the end of this process, after all my "how" questions, my personal application of Proverbs 22:6 would be as follows. In order for me to be a parent who is faithful to teach her children about the Bible and the God it's about, I need to let my children see how the Word of God has transformed me in the areas I struggle most. Personally, for me, that area where I need the most transformation is in my emotions - anger, pride, all those prickly things that bubble to the surface when you add a little dash of kids to the mix.

When my kids see such a transformation as brought about by the Word and will of God, I will trust God with the results of my faithfulness. I will trust him with the future and fate of my child.

Notice I've answered the "What do I do?" question: I am to immerse myself in God's Word so that it transforms me. And I've got a concrete (not vague) application: I need to cooperate with the Spirit as his Word transforms my emotions.

So far I've asked two very general "how" questions in applying Proverbs 22:6. If I stop the application process at this point, I will have short-circuited the work of God's Word in my life. Next, I must ask myself how I can apply the principle of the passage to the area in my life that needs it most – my emotions. Specifically, how do I cooperate with the Spirit as his Word transformations my heart and sinful emotions? I cannot be a biblically faithful parent until I honestly identify those sinful emotions and why I am feeling them. Those emotions start with my own heart, and part of my challenge to remain faithful to God's Word is to surrender and confess to him those sinful desires of my heart that I have elevated to a demand. Applying Proverbs 22:6 starts with my own heart – identifying and confessing sin and trusting the Spirit to further convict my heart as I go about each day parenting my boys.

As you look at Proverbs 22:6, your application is likely different from mine. That is precisely the point! This is why I say results may vary because the Spirit may show you something different from what he is showed me. The principles of a passage never change, but in our day, our context, our personal lives, the specific application of that principle will vary.

Just remember that the most helpful element in determining how to apply a passage is to pepper the principle behind the passage with "how" questions. Start with the heart question, which is where God starts, and work out from there. In application, we are moving from general to specific, from past (interpretation) to present.

The "how" questions will be your most helpful tools in applying God's Word while avoiding lazy religion and legalistic religion. They act as a helpful guide as you seek to discover "what am I supposed to do, Lord?"

In Bible study, we are not looking to find and live by a to-do list that makes us acceptable in God's sight; rather, we are striving after spiritual health brought on by true heart change. God's Word is powerful, dynamic, and trustworthy. His Spirit illuminates our understanding and equips us as we seek to obey it. And at the end of that process, we will be changed.

CONCLUSION

God's Word is his personal Word to you. He designed it to be enjoyed in such a way that your life will forever be marked and changed by it. When we are careful to study and apply his Word to our unique circumstances and seasons of life, we will end up looking like and living like our King. If our studies together in Psalm 19 have shown us anything, it's that we come away from God's Word changed women when we've approached them in the right way.

God's Word changes our whole being – our desires, thoughts, emotions, and behaviors. You can probably already see where this train is headed. Yes, sometimes this transformation process is painful. There are times I come away from the Scriptures with such an over-whelming sense of my own sinfulness that I am forced to surrender all my worries and fears to his cross. Sometimes we carry feelings like shame and guilt around for so long that they begin to function like an extra appendage; they become a part of who we are. So, when we are asked to surrender them, it seems like we've been asked to cut off an arm. But to continue to nurse and cling to them would mean even greater sor-row in that we would experience life's lowest moments apart from the Spirit's peace and joy.

Similarly, countless times I have come away from my morning devotions having heard the Spirit whisper gently to my heart calling me to obey or respond by 'doing' something for his glory – whether its teaching a Bible study, apologizing to a family member, going on a mission trip, meeting a physical need, or simply reaching out to someone who has been marginalized. God's Word calls us to both be acted upon by his Spir-it and act as a result of his Spirit in our lives. Both are hard. Both take trust.

Truly, God's Word is our secret ingredient to living a joyful, meaningful, and victorious life. It is not a deli-cacy reserved for the holy or privileged few, but given freely for all to feast upon. This is the measure of his grace and mercy toward us in Christ Jesus (Eph. 2:6-10). Let us become women of the Word who crave God's Word above all else in the world because we truly know it to be sweeter than honey.

But more than what we get out of God's Word is the motivation of whom we receive. When we read God's Word we come face to face with the God of the Universe himself, the Living Word, our Shield and Reward. Diligent study of the Scriptures requires that I reset my perceptions of who God is. His Word tells us clearly about his nature and his activity in us and in the world. It acts as a natural remedy to the fuzzy definitions offered by the world or conjured by my sinful heart.

Thankfully, our God never leaves us alone in this task of observing, interpreting, and applying his Word to our lives. His Spirit is ever present in those who belong to him, helping us to listen and learn and love like him. Still today, there are passages and parts of Scripture that I find difficult or that I have learned to yield back to him, knowing that one day, I will behold him in all his fullness with great rejoicing instead of fear. When that final day comes, and his kingdom feast is upon us, I don't want to be caught unprepared or ill-equipped. I want to be made ready through the Word. I want to be ready to inherit his kingdom and to be his special inheritance (1 Pet. 2:9).

Come, join me at our Master's table. There is always room for more.

7 *The law of the Lord is perfect,*
  reviving the soul;
 the testimony of the Lord is sure,
  making wise the simple;
8 *the precepts of the Lord are right,*
  rejoicing the heart;
 the commandment of the Lord is pure,
  enlightening the eyes;
9 *the fear of the Lord is clean,*
  enduring forever;
 the rules of the Lord are true,
  and righteous altogether.
10 *More to be desired are they than gold,*
  even much fine gold;
 sweeter also than honey
  and drippings of the honeycomb.
11 *Moreover, by them is your servant warned;*
  in keeping them there is great reward.
12 *Who can discern his errors?*
  Declare me innocent from hidden faults.
13 *Keep back your servant also from presumptuous sins;*
  let them not have dominion over me!
 Then I shall be blameless,
  and innocent of great transgression.
14 *Let the words of my mouth and the meditation of my heart*
  be acceptable in your sight,
  O Lord, my rock and my redeemer.

Ps. 19:7-14

CHAPTER 5 DISCUSSION QUESTIONS

1. Where do you tend to get stuck in the craving cycle? Attitude toward God's Word? Appetite for God's Word? Aim of God's Word? What happens when you get stuck? What triggers do you need to watch out for?

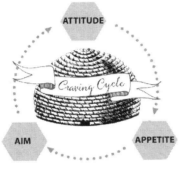

2. Making errors in applying God's Word is a common mistake. Have you ever been guilty of being too specific or too vague in applying a passage in the Bible? If you have a group, share with them how this error was revealed to you and, if appropriate, the consequences of your error.

Based on your observations and inter-pretation (MIT) of Mark 8, how is God prompting you to apply Mark 8:22-25 to your life today? Use the questions below to get you started.

What principle(s) appear in Mark 8:22-25?

HEART QUESTIONS:

How does this principle work in my life?

How can I apply this principle to those areas of my life that are currently lacking?

3. Look over your studies of Mark 8:22-25 conducted throughout this book. How did the OIA model of Bible study (observation, inter-pretation, application) impact your understanding of this passage?

FEAST WITH ME

Part of growing in God's Word is being changed by it – from the inside out. If you are leading a small group, assign one of the following verses to each women to look up and read aloud. Then discuss the heart's role in our spiritual transformation through the Word.

Romans 2:5; 5:5; 10:10

James 4:1-10

Hebrews 4:12-13

Psalms 51:10-12

Jeremiah 17:9-10; 24:7; 29:13

Ezekiel 36:26-27

Are you ready to *change* what you *crave*?

31-DAY *Bible Reading* CHALLENGE

BEE INTENTIONAL • BEE ACCOUNTABLE • BEE CHANGED

Cultivate an appetite for God's Word by taking the #SweeterthanHoney 31-Day Bible Reading Challenge. Read one chapter of Matthew each day for 31 days using the OIA model (observation, interpretation, application). Matthew is a great book for introducing new students to the practice of consistent Bible reading. See a sample schedule at the end of the book. Consider these tips as you proceed:

Bee Intentional - Download and print 31 copies of my free Bible study template before the challenge starts. Pick a consistent time and place to read each day. Set your alarm and prep your coffee the evening before, so getting up early to read is easier. If you miss a day, don't try to make up reading. The sample schedule has several catch-up reading days built in. There are no judgments for missed days, just a willingness to read and study God's Word as you can.

Bee Accountable - Create a private Facebook group and invite friends or your discipleship group to take the challenge together. Each day, post a quick check-in for accountability such as, "I'm up and reading!" or "I read this morning!" If you want to engage further, post an observation, a question about interpretation, or cries for help! Select a leader to facilitate discussion and encourage your group along the way. (Disciplers, this is a great challenge to undertake with someone you are discipling!)

Bee Hopeful - Trust that God will move during this time. Expect to hear from him and expect to be changed by his Word! Be sure to share how God is at work in you with others! Nothing encourages women more than seeing and hear how God is at work in the lives of others.

SAMPLE READING SCHEDULE:

Day 1: Matt. 1	Day 17: Matt. 15
Day 2: Matt. 2	Day 18: Matt. 16
Day 3: Matt. 3	Day 19: Matt. 17
Day 4: Matt. 4	Day 20: Matt. 18
Day 5: Matt. 5	Day 21: Matt. 19
Day 6: Matt. 6	Day 22: Matt. 20
Day 7: Matt. 7	Day 23: Matt. 21
Day 8: CATCH-UP	Day 24: CATCH-UP
Day 9: Matt. 8	Day 25: Matt. 22
Day 10: Matt. 9	Day 26: Matt. 23
Day 11: Matt. 10	Day 27: Matt. 24
Day 12: Matt. 11	Day 28: Matt. 25
Day 13: Matt. 12	Day 29: Matt. 26
Day 14: Matt. 13	Day 30: Matt. 27
Day 15: Matt. 14	Day 31: Matt. 28
Day 16: CATCH-UP	

FREE BIBLE STUDY TEMPLATE

Available for download at:
www.hiveresources.com/books/sweeterthanhoney

TASTING THE SWEETNESS
OF OUR SAVIOR

You might be one of many women for whom life has proven to be anything but sweet, and you're probably wondering what this little book I wrote can offer you. Trust me when I say, not much. I can't offer you anything, but I know Someone who can. His name is Jesus, and he loves you very much. He knows first hand that life can be a bitter pill to swallow. It might surprise you to know that there is little in your life he hasn't already experienced – betrayal, rejection, mocking, beatings, shame, extreme emotional duress, abandonment, loss, wrath, and even death.

Even though he willingly walked in these circumstances, this is not the sweet life he intended for you or for me. Before you were born, before the world was created even, God desired you to live a life of blessing with him in his kingdom. He created you and me for a special purpose, putting us in charge of his kingdom. When others looked at us, he wanted them to see in us his glory and grace just by the way we lived our lives. But with the entrance of sin into the world through our first parents (Adam and Eve), sin corrupted God's good design, bringing with it all the pain and bitterness you now live out and see around you. Instead of the sweet life, we live broken lives. It all started when we rebelled against God's throne, setting ourselves up as the monarch of our lives. Instead of ruling with God in righteousness, we have become an enemy of his throne – separated from him and his blessings. Yet instead of banishing us from his kingdom, the King chose to pardon us. The King sent his only Son to pay the penalty for our rebellion – dying on the cross in our place and bearing the Father's wrath in our stead. As a result, God transferred all our sins to his sinless Son and credited to us all the Son's righteousness.

This is indeed good news! Our ledger of sin has been cleared, erased, and is remembered by God no more. But the sweetness of our Savior does not end there. For on the third day following his death, God raised his Son from the grave, an event witnessed by many and recorded in the Scriptures. Through Christ's resurrection, all life's bitter pills - death and sorrow and sin - were defeated once and for all. In Christ, the Father not only pardons us, but paints for us a picture of the new type of life he invites us to enjoy through him – a Spirit-filled, gospel-empowered life. The world may be bitter, but our Savior is sweet, and he begs us come and taste of himself for ourselves.

One day, all bitterness will be eradicated forever. Christ promises he will complete his kingdom and his work of salvation in you. At that time, we will look like him and live like him completely – like the kings and queens he created us to be. In him, he has given us a special seat of honor at a feast he is preparing for all those who love him, even now. The knowledge that life as we know it is not the end means we can experience joy and peace today, but even more so on the day we feast with him in his new kingdom.

Although his lavish table is open to all, our place at the feast will only be secured if we R.S.V.P. in advance. To enjoy the sweetness of the Savior, we must accept his invitation. Accepting his invitation is as simple as A.B.C.

A - First, we must *acknowledge our sin* and our need for a Savior. Sin is a heart problem, so there is no use in trying to clean ourselves up first or trying to look our best before him. We need a new heart, one that only he can give. We must come to him with the humble recognition that we are not enough, but he is. Rom. 3:23: *"For all have sinned and fall short of the glory of God."*

B – Second, we must *believe that Jesus Christ paid the penalty for our sin* when he died on the cross and that through his resurrection we come to live the full life he envisioned for us from the very beginning. It is by his work alone that we are saved from sin and its effects. Rom. 6:23: *"For the wages of sin is death, but the free gift of God is eternal life in Christ Jesus our Lord."*

C – Third, we must *confess Jesus as our Lord and King*. Confess means we turn over the steering wheel of our life to him, without backseat driving! In order to do so, we must dethrone all those lesser kings in our lives (self-promotion, independence, comfort, pride, acceptance, money) and enthrone him instead. We make him Lord when we seek to follow his will through his

Word. 1 John 31:9: "*If we confess our sins, he is faithful and just to forgive us our sins and to cleanse us from all unrighteousness.*"

A. B. C. This is what it means to taste and to experience first hand the sweet grace and mercy of our King. It is he who sets the divine table and begs us to eat at great expense to himself - it cost him his own life and breath and blood. No finer table have you seen; he has spared no expense. All this waits for you. So, come. Eat. Feast on his grace and mercy. Only through him will you find that life can truly be sweet – both in this life and the next.

> "*Oh, taste and see that the Lord is good!*
> *Blessed is the man who takes refuge in him!*"
> Psalm 34:8

SWEET RESOURCES

DeYoung, Kevin. Taking God At His Word: Why the Bible is Knowable, Necessary, and Enough, and What That Means for You and Me (Wheaton: Crossway, 2014).

Ferguson, Sinclair. From the Mouth of God: Trusting, Reading, and Applying the Bible (East Peoria: Banner of Truth, 2014).

Geisler, Norman and William Nix. A General Introduction to the Bible (Chicago: Moody Press, 1986).

Hendricks, Howard. Living By the Book (Chicago: Moody Publishers, 2007).

Komoszewski, Ed J., James Sawyer, and Daniel Wallace. Reinventing Jesus: How Contemporary Skeptics Miss the Real Jesus and Mislead Popular Culture (Grand Rapids: Kregel Publications, 2006).

Sailhamer, John H. NIV Compact Bible Commentary (Grand Rapids: Zondervan, 1994).

Saucy, Robert. Scripture: Its Power, Authority, and Relevance (Nashville: Thomas Nelson, 2001).

Roberts, Vaughan. God's Big Picture: Tracing the Storyline of the Bible (Downers Grove: Intervarsity Press, 2002).

Wilkin, Jen. Women of the Word: Studying the Bible with Both Our Hearts and Our Minds (Wheaton: Crossway, 2014).

To view and learn more about the Dead Sea Scrolls, visit http://www.deadseascrolls.org.il/.

DAUGHTERS OF THE KING

A 10-lesson Bible study for anyone struggling
to find themselves on the pages of God's Word

Daughters of the King *is a
book for any woman who
has struggled to understand
the central meaning of
Scripture and how it all fits
together. This study offers a
systematic look at how the
Bible is arranged around the
topic of God's kingdom and
how God's kingdom applies
to women today.*

Also available in Kindle & hardcopy
amazon.com

Introducing...

the first in a discipleship series for **unchurched** women

Crowned: Created For Glory, Called By His Name is a concise five-week discipleship guide designed to to help women lacking a biblical background learn to root her identity in Christ.

Each chapter uncovers the significance of one of five salvation truths by answering two key questions: *Who is God?* and *Who am I in Christ?*

- ▶ Creation
- ▶ Redemption
- ▶ Justification
- ▶ Adoption
- ▶ Sanctification

From each of these truths concerning the character and activity of God, a disciple can step into her

kingdom destiny...

who she is in Christ and how she's meant to live in a modern world.

ABOUT THE AUTHOR

MELISSA DEMING is the author of *Daughters of the King: Finding Your Place in the Biblical Story* and the creator of hiveresources.com - a site to help women sweeten their walk with Christ. She and her husband, Jonathan, have identical twins, Zacharias and Jonah. Melissa has a M.Div. in Women's Studies from Southeastern Baptist Theological Seminary, Wake Forest, N.C., and a B.A. in Journalism from Texas A&M University.

ABOUT THE ARTIST

ELLIE BENSON

is an artist and designer and occasional writer living in Augusta, GA. She and her husband, Kenneth, have two lovely daughters, Emma and Alice. She writes on art, faith, and family at ellieeugenia.com.

NOTES

[1] You will find that the more you dig into God's Word, the more tools you need. My time in seminary changed how I view the Bible, so I know how important education truly is with respect to learning how to handle God's Word. I encourage all women who desire to know God more deeply through his Word to research your higher education options for Bible training.

[2] Lewis, C.S., *Reflections on the Psalms: The Celebrated Musings on one of the Most Intriguing Books of the Bible,* (Mariner Books: New York, 2012), 63.

[3] When evangelical scholars speak of the Word of God, they are referring to the 66 books of the Bible, Genesis to Revelation. Only these 66 books have been weighed and confirmed to be the Word of God to men and, as such, are included in the canon of the Scriptures. Other traditions include more. Outside Christianity, some religious groups make a similar claim, believing their holy books to have a divine origin. This book will unpack the biblical claim that the One True God has spoken and speaks exclusively through the Bible.

[4] Derek Kidner, *Tyndale Old Testament Commentaries*, "Psalms 1-72," (Downers Grove, IL: IVP Academic), 117.

[5] Kidner, 117.

[6] Ibid.

[7] Kevin DeYoung, *Taking God at His Word: Why the Bible is Knowable, Necessary, and Enough, and What that Means for You and Me*" (Wheaton: Crossway Books, 2014), 44-45.

[8] "The State of the Bible 2014," is available for download at:
http://www.americanbible.org/uploads/content/state-of-the-bible-data-analysis-american-bible-society-2014.pdf

[9] DeYoung, 37.

[10] Eichenwalk, Kurt, "The Bible: So Misunderstood It's a Sin." *Newsweek* (Winter 2014),

http://www.newsweek.com/2015/01/02/thats-not-what-bible-says-294018.html (accessed May 20, 2016).

[11] Chart reproduced from Komoszewski, J. Ed., *Reinventing Jesus: What the DaVinci Code and Other Novel Speculations Don't Tell You* (Kregel: Grand Rapids, 2006), 71.

[12] Komoszewski, 75.

[13] You can view the Dead Sea Scrolls at:

http://www.deadseascrolls.org.il/home.

[14] Geisler, Norman and William Nix, *A General Introduction to the Bible* (Chicago: Moody Press, 1986), 367.

[15] Geisler and Nix, 367. Prior to the Dead Sea Scrolls, Hebrew texts were based on the Masoretic Text (MT) of which the earliest copy dated to 900 A.D. The MT was the primary source of the Hebrew OT we have. The discovery of the Dead Sea scrolls proved the Masorites (scribes interested in preserving ancient Judaism – both language and culture) were indeed careful in copying the biblical texts. The Masorites were responsible for adopting transmission strategies such as vowel pointing (dots written above and below the text) so as not to add or take away from the text. They also created a system based on identifying the center letter of each line. If at the end of the page, the number of letters did not correspond to the original, they destroyed the copy and began anew.

[16] A *General Introduction to the Bible* by Norman Geisler and Nix and *Reinventing Jesus* by J. Ed Komoszewski both outline the canonization process.

[17] Komoszewki, 130-132. As early as 140 A.D., we see "canon" lists beginning to circulate among the early church. One was the Muratorian Canon (2nd Century) which listed about 22 New Testament books. By the 4th century (367 A.D.), the canon was officially closed – meaning no additional books were deemed as Scripture. But even from the early church to the 4th century, the same books were discussed – the 27 books of the

NT – not any other gospels or apocalypses.

[18] For more on Jesus' view of the Bible, see Matt. 21:42, 22:29, 26:54, 56; John 2:22, 5:39, 10:35; Luke 24:32, 44. (Cf: Acts 17:2; 2 Cor. 4:2; Heb. 4:12; Rev. 1:2).

[19] For a look at shifts in worldviews, see Genn S. Sunshine's book, *Why You Think the Way You Do: The Story of Western Worldviews From Home to Rome* (Zondervan, Grand Rapids, 2009).

[20] "The State of the Bible 2014," available for download at: http://www.americanbible.org/uploads/content/state -of-the-bible-data-analysis-american-bible-society-2014.pdf.

[21] Case in point is D.F. Swabb's book *We Are Our Brains: A Neurobiography of the Brain, from the Womb to Alzheimer's* (Spiegel & Grau), 2014.

[22] VanGemeren, Willem A. "II. The Revelation of God's Law (19:7-11)" In *The Expositor's Bible Commentary*: Volume 5. 182. Grand Rapids: Zondervan Publishing House, © 1991.

[23] Spurgeon, Charles, *The Treasury of David: Vol. 1* (Zondervan: Grand Rapids, 1975), 273.

[24] Mychaskiw, Marianne, "Report: Women Spend an Average of $15,000 on Makeup in Their Lifetimes," *InStyle* (April 17, 2013),

http://www.instyle.com/beauty/15-under-15-best-bargain-beauty-products (accessed May 20, 2016).

[25] O'Brien, Elizabeth, "10 secrets of the anti-aging industry" *Market Watch* (February 13, 2014), http://www.marketwatch.com/story/10-things-the-anti-aging-industry-wont-tell-you-2014-02-11 (accessed May 20, 2016).

[26] Phillips, John, *Exploring the Psalms: Vol. 1* (Loizeaux Brothers: New Jersey, 1988), 152.

[27] Phillips, 152.

[28] *Gesenius Hebrew Chaldee Lexicon*, s.v. "innocent," https://www.blueletterbible.org/lang/lexicon/lexicon.cfm?Strongs=H5352&t=NKJV (accessed May 20, 2016).

[29] Hendricks, Howard, *Living by the Book*, (Chicago: Moody Press, 1991), 19.

[30] Lifeway has a colored chart that illustrates the divisions of the Old and New Testament. http://www.lifeway.com/Product/wall-chart-books-of-the-bible-P001153715. They also have a helpful graphic posted on their blog at: http://blog.lifeway.com/explorethebible/downloads/genres-of-biblical-literature/.

[31] Although I always revered the Word of God, it wasn't until I read through the second half of the book of Isaiah and discovered the depth of its prophecy (it speaks specifically of the coming Christ 400 years be-

fore he actually arrived) that I became enthralled with the *message* of the Scriptures. The more I studied the structure of the Bible (how it was put together), the more enthralled I became with its *beauty*. For instance, did you know that the entire book of Ruth is written in a literary structure called a chiaism? This structure acts like an accordion; each chapter mirrors each other until the text meets in an apex. This apex serves as the theological key to understand the author's message. This is a lofty and skilled literary form found in very few pieces of ancient literature. The literary beauty of the Bible is unparalleled. Most importantly, however, the more I have learned to feast on the Word, the more I have come to enjoy its *effects* – its transformative power on the human body and soul. When we lived in overseas, we had the privilege to walk several friends through the story of the Scriptures, and we were given a front-row seat as the Bible changed our friends from the inside out.

[32] Hendricks, 47-50.

[33] Blue Letter Bible has a helpful list of the names of God. Visit:
https://www.blueletterbible.org/search/Dictionary/viewTopic.cfm?topic=IT0003853.

[34] Olive Tree Bible software has an excellent summary chart of parts of speech and verb tenses including examples at:
http://otapp3.olivetree.com/learningcenter/articles/grammar.php.

[35] Here's an example of diagramming using, Logos Bible Software: https://youtu.be/ElsXOE5JQAY.

[36] For some additional pointers on making charts and creating lists, see Hendricks, 182-189.

[37] DeYoung, 69.

[38] Hendricks, 197.

[39] VanGemeren, Willem A. "Psalm 21: The Rule of God Through His King" In *The Expositor's Bible Commentary*: Volume 5. 192. Grand Rapids: Zondervan Publishing House, © 1991.

[40] Hendricks, 127.

[41] Daniel Akin, "Main Idea of the Text" (unpublished class notes for BTI5000 Hermeneutics), Southeastern Baptist Theological Seminary, 2009.

[42] Akin, "Main Idea of the Text."

[43] Akin, "Main Idea of the Text."

Made in the USA
Las Vegas, NV
13 October 2022

57201638R00103